MARKETPLACE
MULTIPLIERS

STORIES OF FAITH AND
INFLUENCE IN THE WORKPLACE

WITH DAVID DRURY

ILLUSTRATED BY LUIS CHÁVEZ

wesleyan
PUBLISHING HOUSE
wphstore.com
Fishers, Indiana

Published by Wesleyan Publishing House
Fishers, Indiana 46037
Printed in the United States of America
ISBN: 978-1-63257-441-1
ISBN (e-book): 978-1-63257-442-8

Names: Drury, David, 1974- compiler.
Title: Marketplace multipliers : stories of faith and influence in the
   workplace / with David Drury ; illustrated by Luis Chavez.
Description: Fishers, Indiana : Wesleyan Publishing House, [2021] |
   Summary: "Marketplace Multipliers includes stories of seventeen
   Christians who have been unleashed to have an outsized God-blessed
   influence on the world around them as they intentionally focus on
   integrating faith and work, making disciples, and multiplying the
   kingdom in the marketplace"-- Provided by publisher.
Identifiers: LCCN 2020045515 (print) | LCCN 2020045516 (ebook) | ISBN
   9781632574411 | ISBN 9781632574428 (ebook)
Subjects: LCSH: Employees--Religious life--Biography. | Evangelistic work.
   | Work environment. | Influence (Psychology)--Religious
   aspects--Christianity. | Work--Religious aspects--Christianity.
Classification: LCC BV4593 .M28 2021 (print) | LCC BV4593 (ebook) | DDC
   248.8/80922--dc23
LC record available at https://lccn.loc.gov/2020045515
LC ebook record available at https://lccn.loc.gov/2020045516

Illustrations by Luis Chávez

CONTENTS

Foreword   5

Introduction   9

1. The Influence of Excellent Service   13
   —Carrie J. Whitcher

2. Nurse and Pastor   21
   —Rochelle Jenkins

3. Audience of One   31
   —Paul Anthes

4. God's Hustler   39
   —Damon Thrash

5. A Lifetime of Quality Care   49
   —Gary Ott

6. The Gift of Living the Great Commission   59
   —Ben Paulsen

7. Going Pro for a Purpose   69
   —Evan Maxwell

8. Pray for the Unexpected   77
   —Diane Foley

9. Faith and Logic   85
   —Philip Farrell

10. One Life   97
    —Yaremí Alicea-Morales

11. Discipleship in Every Opportunity   103
    —Julia Pyle

12. Ministry through Finance   111
     —Pete Benson

13. Faith Is Not Just for Sundays   119
     —Trent Dailey

14. Prayer Opens Doors   127
     —Wafaa Hanna

15. Adore the Blesser   135
     —Omar Haedo

16. Influence through Healing   145
     —Scott Addison

17. Lead Differently   151
     —Estherlita Griffiths

Appendix 1A: Starting Your Own Local Chapter of
Marketplace Multipliers: Summary   159

Appendix 1B: Starting Your Own Local Chapter of
Marketplace Multipliers: Details   163

Appendix 2A: Starting Your Own Gathering at Work:
Summary   173

Appendix 2B: Starting Your Own Gathering
at Work: Details   177

About the Authors   187

FOREWORD

I'm a raving fan of people who live out their faith in the marketplace. They prayerfully seek to integrate their faith with their work and steward their influence upon others. Whatever the context of their work, they want God's light to shine through them.

This goes deep for me. My dad owned a construction business and I started working for him when I was twelve. He was a "man after God's own heart," whether at home, at church, or at work and was known for his integrity and excellence in his work. His life for Jesus deeply impressed me and countless others who witnessed his integrity; however, he graciously made it clear that it was not just because he was a great guy, but because he had been transformed when he committed himself to Christ in his twenties.

I began college as a business major. My dream was to build the family business into a development company. My entrepreneurial wiring fit the dream, which included how relationships and resources in the marketplace could be used by God. My struggle in surrendering to God's call to vocational ministry was lamenting the loss of ministry opportunities in the marketplace. I have loved the life God has given me as a pastor and as a seminary and denominational leader—and I am grateful that my entrepreneurial bent found a place in those roles. But my heart leaps when I get to be around those who work outside religious institutions, and I desire to see them influence those whose faith journey would never begin, or even deeply continue, in primarily religious organizations.

For over thirty-five years, my accountability partner and I have met every two weeks. Paul is a deeply devoted follower of Christ, called to minister in and through the business he owns. He is passionate about a deep and daily walk with Jesus. His sense of calling to be a disciple that makes disciples is every bit as compelling for him as a lay person as it is for me as clergy. He has influence with people and in places I never will.

So this book of stories of "marketplace multipliers" (MMs) inspires me. What a variety of positions, work environments, passions, and personalities! These women and men differ in generations, ethnicities, and financial means. As you read, mark the ones you most relate to, but don't dismiss what you might learn from people very different from you.

Some of these MMs feel called to encourage others. And some pastors have a desire to bless MMs for how they serve beyond the walls of the church. Now we're connecting the two. You'll learn a bit about this emerging movement just beginning to spread around the world.

I pray that you'll finish this book with a sense of celebration for the immense variety of people and places where God is at work and with a growing awareness that serving in the marketplace is a calling from God also. We will never have a movement of God unless disciples are made in everyday places where we work and relate. The church has left the building! Every person is both called and empowered for kingdom contribution!

—Wayne Schmidt
General Superintendent of The Wesleyan Church

INTRODUCTION

You have more influence than you think. This influence travels wherever you go, and it is not restricted to where you worship. In fact, the vast majority of the influence of Christ in the world today is in marketplace settings—out in public—since the vast majority of Christians go to work every day around the globe.

Marketplace Multipliers includes stories of seventeen Christians who have been unleashed to have an outsized God-blessed influence on the world around them as they intentionally focus on integrating faith and work, making disciples, and multiplying the kingdom in the marketplace.

You will read the dynamic story of Damon, a hustler who spent years in a prison in Florida where his business dreams began; Ben, the man who found himself in a country halfway around the world in Central Asia; Diane, the doctor who found herself working in a US government agency in Washington, DC; and Evan, who as a young man, got a contract to play on a professional basketball team in Eastern Europe. Each person found themselves in unique and unexpected places of influence. You will hear from health care professionals Wafaa, Scott, Julia, and Rochelle, who integrate their faith in everyday conversations with patients and coworkers, engaging in redemptive relationships and vital ministry. You'll find stories from Estherlita, Phil, Carrie, and Yaremi, who hadn't thought they could minister outside of church walls at first but dove into a calling of living transparently with those they work with in order to further the love of Christ. You will hear from Paul, Trent, Gary, Pete, and Omar, who all surrendered their idea of success and control over to God and experienced growth not only in their spiritual lives and relationships, but also in their business ventures. These are the names and stories you'll find as you launch into *Marketplace Multipliers* that are meant to inspire you and provide examples to learn from.

You can do this too. It is not for the super-Christians, the super-wealthy, or the super-gifted. Your multiplier influence can be used by God for good whether you work in business, health care, education, media, community service, government, or any other kind of work. Even if you are retired or don't draw a paycheck from outside the home, God has a place for you to use your influence for him. In these pages, you'll discover ways to make a difference too, and it all starts with unleashing your God-given design and following the Holy Spirit's lead in your world.

As you invest in these stories, take time to reflect on the questions at the end of each chapter so that you can be inspired to:

- Discover what being a Christian influencer in the world around you looks like and how you see yourself in that role;

- Determine where you would like to be in the future as a marketplace multiplier;
- Gain a sense of blessing, release, and anointing for the influence you have;
- Lean into opportunities to use your skills, connections, and resources more intentionally to improve and extend the work of the church into the world around you.

For more resources and to get connected to the marketplace multipliers community, visit MarketplaceMultipliers.com.

1
THE INFLUENCE OF EXCELLENT SERVICE

CARRIE J. WHITCHER

> *Shortly before dawn Jesus went out to them, walking on the lake. . . . "Come," [Jesus] said. Then Peter got down out of the boat, walked on the water and came toward Jesus.*
> —Matthew 14:25–29

I grew up with a younger sister who has special needs. As a young girl, I remember when the two of us and all my friends were running through our backyard. I wrestled with an internal struggle, trying to decide whether I would run ahead with my friends so I could be included with them, or stay behind with my sister since she would never be able to keep up. I feared that my friends would think I was slow and not worth waiting for. But, even as a small child, I knew I made the right choice as I stayed back with my sister.

Fortunately, my friends realized that my sister needed me more. They understood her need, especially since her disability was visible and she needed additional support.

I felt I needed to put my energy, time, and focus on her. These kinds of experiences at a very young age taught me that caring for others was more important than caring about what others were thinking.

Of course, at the time I didn't know it was preparing me for who I am and what I do today. It helped me to become constantly aware and intentionally mindful of the needs of the people around me, which became central to my life and work. My eyes were opened to things that I would not have seen otherwise.

In my current role, I have the opportunity to influence 1.5 million people across upstate New York in improving their health care. This early upbringing with my sister has become core to my leadership life, whether it involves bringing diversity to the team, or ensuring that those with differing opinions have a voice. My desire to help and serve others is hardwired as I seek to influence ongoing quality improvement in our health care system.

Learning to think of my sister's inclusion, worrying about her health, and ensuring she received the care that she needed inspired me to do what I do today—lead a team of talented clinicians, analysts, project managers, and health care advocates who work with patients by empowering them to improve their health in ways they want and need.

A SOLID FOUNDATION TO BECOMING A MARKETPLACE MULTIPLIER

I witnessed leadership and faith at a very young age. My parents were Sunday school teachers, my father was an Episcopal churchwarden, and my grandfather was a pastor. I was also raised in a musical family and came to love music at an early age. I remember my grandfather asking me to play "O Holy Night" on my flute at his Christmas Eve service year after year and asking me to join him at church services at the nursing home with my flute and guitar.

When I was nine years old, I attended a church youth camp. I had a counselor by the name of Christine who poured into me while I was there, and at that time I accepted Jesus into my heart in a very personal way, beyond what my family had already taught me.

Later, following my graduate education, I had the opportunity to serve in a leadership role at a nursing home in order to care for people and improve their lives. It helped me realize I could have an influence on a whole culture—a whole organization—and improve outcomes for those I served every day. When I went to work for a health insurance company, I began to think of deploying some of the same quality improvement methodologies that I had used in the nursing home. People usually don't think of a health insurance company improving the quality of health care, but that was very much my calling and the company's mission. This role was a new opportunity to work with our hospitals and physicians' offices to drive quality improvement for our patients. I've been able to influence that for sixteen years and now oversee corporate-wide quality improvement strategies and programs across our health plan.

As I've done this, I have attempted to become more intentional in how I integrate not only my childhood experiences, but also my faith in my work. I've had a staff person tell me, "You put the team and the needs of our patients ahead of your needs, really ahead of what you want." That's exactly the example I want to set. That, I feel, is the way Jesus would function in this same role. I want to pour into people and disciple them in this quality improvement journey.

My pastor, Ken, helped me grow in my awareness of how to be visible as a Christian in the marketplace. Quite honestly, I did not truly see it until he connected the dots. I think every minister has a role to help those in their church serve others in the marketplace, to help them see the unique influence they have, and to help them move beyond being just "Sunday Christians."

I began to see my role as that of a "marketplace multiplier." I realized that in my capacity, I can equip Christians to influence their workplace and integrate their faith by making disciples and unleashing the kingdom of God, wherever they are. This means being intentional in integrating my faith and work to the benefit of those around me in my workplace. It means moving beyond church walls and ensuring I am intentional about using my influence to make disciples and multiply the kingdom of God. Any Christian can do this in whatever career or areas of influence they are led into. I have no doubt that God is always at work where we work, so we serve the higher interests of the kingdom while leading with excellence in the marketplace.

When it comes down to it, building lasting relationships is foundational to what I do and what marketplace multipliers do. That means connecting with people who work for me, work across from me as peers, and are higher than me in the organization. These relationships become true equal partnerships when I get to know them deeply, understand their wiring and what drives them, and share the same about myself. In these relationships, our faith exudes and we partner together in new ways, find new strength, and support one another in bold ways that pour into each other when needed most.

My desire to help and serve others is hardwired as I seek to influence ongoing quality improvement in our health care system.

/ / / / / / / / / / / / / / / / /

The scene in Scripture that influences my thinking of this the most is when Jesus bids Peter to "Come to me," while walking on the water in Matthew 14. Like Peter, I have to step out of the boat and do something that doesn't even seem to make sense at first. Even in the middle of the storm and standing on the water—like Peter—I must look at Jesus in the distance. If Peter had kept his eyes on Jesus and continued to trust him, he could have run across that water and embraced Jesus. Instead, he doubted for a moment and then went under and Jesus had to save him. Of course, Peter was the only one who stepped out of the boat in the first place.

/ /

I want to have that "stepping outside the boat" kind of faith and boldness in my relationships.

The song "Oceans (Where Feet May Fail)" by Hillsong has inspired me in that direction.[1]

You call me out upon the waters
The great unknown where feet may fail . . .

And I will call upon Your name
And keep my eyes above the waves
When oceans rise, my soul will rest in Your embrace . . .

Spirit lead me where my trust is without borders . . .

Like Peter, Jesus calls me out onto the waters of the great unknown where my feet may fail. But if I keep my eyes above the waves when oceans rise, my soul will rest in his embrace. If I can do that out here in the marketplace, I know that the Spirit will lead me where my trust is without borders and where I can walk on the waters. That's my prayer, because I believe I can do all things through Christ who strengthens me (see Phil. 4:13) as I function with Christ's resurrection power.

VALUE STATEMENTS INFLUENCED BY FAITH

The influence I can have in the organization is not limited to just those whom I have relationships with. Our organization has gone through a cultural transformation, and I have been able to influence and fully engage in that process. Our CEO was very intentional in developing specific value statements and related behaviors that drove an expectation for how we work every day. Whether you are a leader in our organization, like the CEO, or a frontline staff person working day in and day out with data or with our members, these declarations of intent become critical to how we operate.

Here is a paraphrase of our company's seven value statements that are influenced by faith or at least practiced by those with faith driving them.

- **Passionately serve our customers**—Customers are more than just our members; they are also our vendors and service providers. This particular value statement has always spoken to me and empowered me to do what I do best.
- **Care about each other**—This statement of intent is all about the behaviors associated with being intentional in recognizing each other's individual value and being examples to each other.
- **Be proud of what we do**—We recognize the amount of satisfaction that comes from doing great work.
- **Challenge and empower each other to deliver excellence**—The process of improving and maintaining quality health care requires that we act with a sense of urgency and listen attentively to the ideas of others to continually improve.
- **Embrace and drive change**—If we keep doing the same things we did yesterday, we are not going to see different results tomorrow. If we want better results, we have to continually innovate and do things differently.
- **Have open and honest conversations**—We need to transparently share our struggles, hold difficult conversations, encourage personal growth, and celebrate successes.

- **Accomplish our mission and have fun too**—We want to have "can do" attitudes that believe in the impossible, while having fun and driving inspiration along the way.

In my eyes, these statements of intent have provided a foundation by which I can effectively lead and integrate my faith into all that I do every day, benefitting not only the people I serve in my organization, but the millions of members we serve across upstate New York.

INFLUENCING YOUR WORK . . . INTEGRATING YOUR FAITH

- Who are the people in your life that can help you connect your faith and your career?
- What values or mission statements do you use at work or personally and how do they reflect Jesus?

CARRIE J. WHITCHER is the vice president of Health Care Improvement at Excellus BlueCross BlueShield and Universa Healthcare. Before joining Excellus, she served as the administrator of a 320-bed skilled nursing and rehabilitation center. Carrie also served as the president of the Western New York Healthcare Executive Forum, as well as on the board of directors for Watermark Wesleyan Church and Houghton College. Carrie earned a bachelor of science degree in health services administration from the State University of New York College at Fredonia and a master's degree in health services administration from Xavier University in Cincinnati, Ohio. Carrie and her husband, Matthew, reside in Orchard Park, New York, and have two children.

NOTE
1. "Oceans (Where Feet May Fail)," words and music by Matt Crocker, Joel Houston, and Salomon Ligthelm, recorded 2013 on *Zion* by Hillsong UNITED.

2
NURSE AND PASTOR

ROCHELLE JENKINS

*Behold, I stand at the door and knock. If anyone hears
my voice and opens the door, I will come in to
him and eat with him, and he with me.*

—Revelation 3:20 (ESV)

I knew I wanted to be a nurse when I was a young teenager. My plan was to study nursing at the University of Wisconsin, but when I became a Christian at the age of sixteen, my plans shifted. I had a Christian friend who wanted to be a nurse too and she told me about this Christian school called Indiana Wesleyan University. I decided I would go with her—more just to support her—and as soon as I walked on campus, I knew that was exactly where I wanted to be. Those years at a Christian university (which also had a great nursing program) helped me begin to understand what it might mean to start integrating my faith into the nursing profession.

Seven years ago, I moved to Indianapolis and began working in the cardiac progressive care unit. After a year in, I was asked to start training new nurses. That leadership position helped me to get out of my shell. At the same time my husband, Travis, was working at a church in the city and we began thinking intentionally about starting a ministry for young adults. As that was happening, I was getting more and more excited about my faith and it just started to come out of me in my workplace. People would ask me how things were going, and I would share about our church and work.

BREAKING DOWN BARRIERS TO SPIRITUAL CONVERSATIONS

The people I'm working with are crazy busy; most work twelve-hour shifts, both days and nights. Integrating my faith into this kind of setting is different. These people are invested in my life and I'm invested in theirs—we're a team together. Because of this, my faith seeps into our conversations. Rather than one big conversation, it will be little two-minute conversations while we are sitting at the nurses' station. We will be charting about what we have done that shift and then start talking about what's been going on in our personal lives.

These short conversations give me the opportunity to talk about my life and how faith is a big part of it. I'll mention a certain Bible passage or story I've been thinking about or that our church has discussed. It's not unheard of for one to ask a question about what that Scripture means for their life or ask about the things they don't really understand about what I've shared. Not everyone is engaged, but two or three other people will gather around and listen.

Sometimes the doctors come to the nurses' station to do their charting as well. One time, I was talking about some part of the Bible our house church had been focused on, when a doctor, who follows a different religion, walked in. We talked about what faith means for different religions and he shared about Eastern practices of religion. Because of his questions, I got the opportunity to walk through the plan of salvation for Christians and clarify how salvation is not based on a person working harder and harder.

This doctor used an image of a mountain to describe faith. He said that every religion is just trying to get to the top of the same mountain but the path each religion takes may be different. I got to share the Christian perspective that perhaps there is a "mountain," but there is no way to get to the top on our own. There is nothing we can do or way that we can act that will ever be good enough. So Christians ask God at the top to come down to us. This explanation deeply impacted the doctor; he loved this flip of his metaphor. He discussed it with me for a couple weeks afterward. This was a really cool opportunity that I never could have planned beforehand.

Now, if you know me, much of this doesn't match what you might think of me. I'm actually very introverted. I love to observe, learn, and listen. But when I'm in the hospital, I can see how God has shaped me differently within that realm. It feels like a leadership calling in that space. It is not a hospital owned by a religious group, it's a "secular" institution, but through these conversations it has become sacred. There is a difference between what I can share and what I can't share, but in building relationships all those barriers break down.

A CHURCH FOR NURSES

During this season we had a friend named James who had a vision for a collection of house churches called "Living Mission." So we joined that church. It was eye-opening for us and really shaped the way we view what being the church can be like.

Eventually we asked if we could start doing that in our neighborhood because I felt that most of the unchurched nurses that I'd been talking to needed a place where they could come and have conversations tailored to what they've understood and what they need to know. James supported us so we started up a meeting in our home.

For a while, I just talked to other nurses about it, explaining what we were planning and that it was designed specifically with them in mind. They were really anticipating it. A nurse told me, "Rochelle, maybe I would go to church, but I work every single Sunday. And with my profession, you work tons of hours or days, sometimes nights, sometimes you don't get a weekend off for months." And that is when it clicked. I needed a church for them, at a time they could make it. Now we meet on Wednesday nights because we found that the nurses who were Christians all took Sundays off, so many of the unchurched nurses worked Sundays or even all weekend.

We didn't know what to expect but several showed up, and many who showed up had zero knowledge of Christianity. One person did have some background, but because of their superstitious religious upbringing, they thought the Bible was too sacred to touch, open, or read themselves, so they never had any personal connection to it. Because of this, the very first meeting was probably the most basic meeting you could ever have—introducing the Bible. It was a Bible tutorial for people with no church background. I think we forget how much Christians take for granted and doing church this way helped us tailor the experience for those seeking God. If these people ever entered through the door of a church (which would be unlikely) then they would be lost in five minutes and no one would know it. By doing church in an interactive way, we could go at their pace and it's been transformative.

One woman came to the meeting who had been given a Bible from someone else; it was still wrapped in packaging. At that very first house church meeting, she literally opened up a Bible for the first time in her life. That was the starting point. Over the next two years, it was amazing to see how comfortable she became in accessing it personally.

They were so excited to come back for the next meeting to talk more about how God shaped the stories in the Bible and how it was written so long ago but was so applicable to what's going on in our lives today.

Over time, we would just mention in conversation what passages we were talking about and how it applied to our lives and that spread around the hospital. People began to ask questions and the conversations became invitations to join in. In sharing my faith, I have to think about where each person is spiritually and personally because certain styles of evangelism will not work with everyone. Nurses are very detail oriented and focused on their jobs and sometimes they don't have the free time to interact. However, I've found that truly caring about what's going on in their lives makes a big difference.

During all of this, I began to feel a call on my life to study for ministry, so I earned a degree on the side. I don't want it to sound like you have to go back to school for this kind of ministry, but I love education, so I studied hard even though it was a lot to juggle. In the process of becoming an ordained minister, I had to do interviews about my ministry to see if I "passed the test." A question I got often was, "Do you plan on being a full-time pastor or a full-time nurse?" I always answered "yes" because I don't see a division between being a nurse and being a pastor.

I am both a nurse and a pastor now. I pastor while in the hospital as much as I pastor in my house church. That does not mean that I am working eighty hours a week. I am just using the job I have in the hospital while being a full-time pastor.

BUILDING TRUST THROUGH DISCIPLESHIP

At one point, I had a cool opportunity to help transition our hospital to an entirely new building, making sure that all the things were in place for the nurses while maintaining morale. When you have a really big change like that, especially for nurses that had been in the hospital for decades, doing something new is always very scary.

In sharing my faith, I have to think about where each person is spiritually and personally because certain styles of evangelism will not work with everyone.

///////////////

So this idea of creating emotional support, as well as the physical support of moving the hospital, went a long way with people. The transition team held parties, offered snacks, and wrote cards to try to get people on board with what was all going on and help them to see that it was a good change, even though it was hard. As people learned that we actually cared about them, trust quickly followed, and opportunities to meet outside of the hospital opened up as well.

When there are nurses going through a hard time, sometimes we take them out to eat to encourage them. I find it interesting that even though I am so outspoken about my faith and "pastor" people naturally, the hospital chose me to provide support during this transition time. Sharing my faith has made me better at my "day job," not worse, and it has not only been welcomed, but has actually given me more of a platform to care for and lead others. I am so grateful for that opportunity and hope that my experience might be instructive for others that worry about how it will come across in their setting or affect their reputation. If you love people and build relationships with them—where you want what is best for them—faith only helps.

For me, making disciples is all about the long game. I need to be connected over time in people's lives. I think of discipling

///////////////////////////

every person in my circle of influence and I think every Christian can think of it in that way. It's not just discipling those who come to my house church, it's reaching those in the hospital, too. My husband has his own circle of influence and each person in my house church has ones they are equipped to influence for God. They don't have to know everything; I don't know everything either. You can influence people—children, friends, neighbors, or coworkers—wherever you are in your spiritual journey.

TRUST WHERE GOD PLACED YOU

For each person considering their marketplace influence, I would say just trust where God placed you. Trust the people that God has placed around you. Pray that you are given eyes to understand their lives. The first and easiest way to get started is to just interact and sometimes it will have to be outside of work, depending on what your job details are. Take someone out to eat, see where they are at, find out their interests. It doesn't start with preaching or some kind of bold prophetic work. It really starts with, "Hey, what's going on in your life?"

In leading a gathering like we have, we have to be very intentional to bring everything down several notches in formality and tradition. When you're in school or in ministry, you're very used to interacting with Christians who know the same language and use the same phrases. If your circle of influence is in the marketplace, it's a completely different culture and language. Even using words like *salvation* can cause confusion until you explain the meaning. Now, these are very smart people; I'm not demeaning them. But an unchurched nurse might not have the biblical vocabulary you and I have, just like you might not have the medical vocabulary she or he has. I've been able to use words like *freedom* or even *mercy* to describe biblical terms—language that they would understand in their daily life.

While starting a church like this is slow and steady, it does have many advantages. I am actually paid for my work in a way that facilitates ministry, even though the church doesn't pay me. It's a way to plant a church in a marketplace-connected setting, in a neighborhood, and authentically cultivate community. I suppose the only cost for our church is baking some cookies for our meeting, but quite honestly if we didn't have those cookies no one would worry about it. Or someone else would bake them. Those cookies might be a physical way to welcome people who come to our little house church, but it's not why they stay. They stay because they meet Jesus there. He is all the welcome anyone needs.

INFLUENCING YOUR WORK . . . INTEGRATING YOUR FAITH

- How can you make your work place a "sacred" space?
- What is one step you can take in order to deepen your work relationships?

ROCHELLE JENKINS is an RN at Community Hospital East in Indianapolis, working on the cardiac progressive care unit. She is blessed to be married to her husband, Travis, who works in ministry alongside her. They have two snuggly puppies who also think they are part of the church.

3
AUDIENCE OF ONE

PAUL ANTHES

Do nothing out of selfish ambition or vain conceit. Rather, in humility value others above yourselves, not looking to your own interests but each of you to the interests of the others.
—Philippians 2:3–4

I became a Christian after I graduated from college. I had been aware of God and the church—and even attended occasionally, earlier in life—but I really hadn't made a commitment for myself until I was an adult.

I think God wired me in a way that I really want to know the purpose for something. I want to know the *why* behind it. After college I began thinking through a lot of "meaning of life" questions. I wondered about my career and knew that the way the world kept score was simple: money and power. I was attracted to those things and went to business school with the idea of preparing myself to be able to make money and gain power.

The problem was that I knew enough people who had made money and gained power and were still miserable. I intuitively knew there must be more to life, because money and power alone could not be the answer. That started a spiritual journey that caused me to accept Christ. I began regularly attending church for the first time and pursuing a relationship with God.

That was a start, but I made the early mistake of putting my life into compartments. Sundays became about being a Christian, but Monday through Saturday was still all about money and power. I volunteered and served at church and did some great stuff, but I didn't connect the two parts of myself. I hate to say it, but marketplace success was the item in first place and my faith was a close second. I didn't give enough attention to integrating my faith into my work. I wanted to be honest and trustworthy, but I wasn't able to see clearly the role that my faith should have in my work.

I began to realize that God was Lord of every area of my life and I needed to surrender it to him. I had wanted to be a successful businessperson first in life and I wanted to be a Christ follower second. I didn't know what God would do if I surrendered to him. Would I still be successful in the marketplace? It was scary for me to give that up.

I now understand that the order of those two things is absolutely essential. I have to put Christ first and pursue being a successful businessperson second. It took me a decade or more to really learn that lesson and start to put that into practice well.

I founded my own financial advising company in 1998 because I wanted the freedom to serve the best interests of clients without having to please others. In the world of financial services, that can be hard to do. With my firm of ten people, we serve about 180 clients on a fee-only basis. It's a high-service and low-volume business model that was intentionally designed that way. We do in-depth comprehensive planning for our clients, along with institutional investment management for them. I've always enjoyed numbers and the business of money, so having this business has been a dream come true for me, especially because of the way we are able to work from a client-first perspective.

LIVING FOR AN AUDIENCE OF ONE

One of the things that has helped me the most in getting clarity on putting God first and being a businessperson second has been the accountability relationship I've had with my pastor, Wayne Schmidt, for thirty-five years. He went on to become a seminary president and denominational leader, but I knew him as my local church pastor. Our connection grew and I began to talk to him about my struggle to integrate my faith and work.

In part because of accountability, I became a steady reader of the Bible. I've since read the Bible many times and intend to read Scripture every day of my life. At one point, an author I read named Os Guinness helped me realize the idea of "one audience." I want to live life with an audience of one, and that's God. It's God I should look to perform for and no one else.

I was able to connect with a mentor in my life over twenty years ago. He was a devoted Christian and successful in the marketplace. That inspired me and I was really curious about his life. He became an example of someone who put Christ first and was also successful in the marketplace, well respected, and did well at his work.

As I was learning how to integrate my faith and work, I took a class at my church that helped us all see ourselves as "believers enabled as ministers." They had us repeat the phrase "I am a minister." I'll be honest, it felt weird for me to say that, but then I began to see the truth in that statement. No, I'm not ordained by any church or denomination, and I don't work for a nonprofit. However, I wholeheartedly believe I am a minister of the gospel in the marketplace. I don't get a paycheck from a church, but I'm in full-time Christian service because I'm thinking of influencing the world around me for Christ full time. It's not a part-time, Sunday-only thing for me anymore.

One example of a change that I intentionally made was instead of going into a room thinking, "What am I going to gain from this?" I began asking, "Why am I here? What can I do to serve the people in this room?" That's a 180-degree difference in posture and motive. It is trusting that if I put God first, other things are going to fall into place. I believe that in God's economy everybody can win at the same time. My success doesn't come at someone else's expense.

By doing this, I live out what I believe. Do I believe that I can achieve the things I yearn for like success, fulfillment, satisfaction, joy, and contentment by trusting God, or do I believe I can find them in a relationship apart from Christ or doing things separate from his ways? The only way for me to find those things is to live life, and especially do business, in a way that is pleasing to him and consistent with biblical principles. Putting others first by representing their best interests, being transparent, honest, and trustworthy—this is what helps me integrate my faith with my work on a daily basis.

I have a unique view on being a "workplace minister" because for decades my accountability partner was the pastor of a church. I got an inside view of what it looks like to be a pastor in a church, which is a difficult job, even lonely and isolating. I respected his ability to do his job well, and the influence he had in certain arenas.

That's the best way to live—living like Christ. . . . I have implemented this philosophy in my companies by deciding that my own profit should only be pursued as a by-product of doing the right things, for the right reasons, at the right time, with other people, because I'm serving their best interests.

We began to notice that there were settings that I had some authority in and could speak into that he couldn't, and vice versa. In some settings, once I revealed I was a business-person, I lost credibility and influence with some people and he gained it when he said he was a minister. Then there were groups when, as you might imagine, as he revealed he was a pastor of a church, he lost authority and the ability to speak in their lives, and I gained it as a businessperson. I grew to understand that I have a reach that my pastor will never have.

I'll interact with some people in conversations that have the potential to go deep that he won't have, and I need to steward that influence.

After several years of success in my business of investing and wealth management, I started another organization called R3 Coaching. The three Rs stand for doing the right things for the right reasons at the right time. We help people with the best practices of executive coaching by fully integrating faith into all the lessons. We help them do better in all of life and to pursue outcomes that allow them to win at work and win at home. They are then able to be more effective in their jobs and their Christian faith.

Through this, I've been able to share how I've learned not just to integrate biblical principles into my work as values, but also how I share my faith with people. I became inclined to think of it as a parallel to "permission evangelism" after reading a book by Michael Simpson of the same title. I give hints and glimpses of my faith in my personal life as I'm building a relationship with people and I intentionally attempt to read their response to what I am sharing. I've found that sometimes

a person resists the subject, they change the topic, look away, and do something to divert you. When that happens, I don't persist in that moment. If I'm going to have a relationship with this person, I need to take my time. I'm looking for permission to speak into those things. If I push through when I don't have permission, I'm probably doing more harm than good. I continue putting small feelers out there, sharing something about my own life that involves faith, the Bible, or spiritual things. When they respond positively to that, I'll go deeper and share more.

This is important because we serve both Christian and non-Christian clients. We give the same advice to non-Christian clients that we give to Christian clients, of course, most of which comes from the Bible, which is full of so much wise information on finances. Our interactions allow us to have conversations with clients about important things in their lives. These types of interactions build relationships and I look for permission from them to have that spiritual conversation.

LOOKING TO THE INTERESTS OF OTHERS

The words of Philippians 2 have shaped the companies I own and have started, as well as my own way of life. That chapter says that each of us should not look to our own interests but to the interests of others. That's the best way to live—living like Christ. Later in the chapter it says that our attitudes should be the same as that of Christ Jesus. I have implemented this philosophy in my companies by deciding that my own profit should only be pursued as a by-product of doing the right things, for the right reasons, at the right time, with other people, because I'm serving their best interests. If profit is in first place, I will be tempted to compromise my faith in small ways by manipulating people, manipulating situations, and exhibiting other behaviors that are not consistent with my faith.

As success grew, I began to pursue a "parallel track." This led me to divide my normal work week between my core work at the business and ministry activities. Because I am in full-time Christian service, I see my use of time as vocational ministry activities and nonvocational ministry activities, which I refer to as NVMA. I wanted my team at work to see that my work in the business is ministry just like serving on the board of a non-profit, volunteering at my church, mentoring, or other activities.

This means I need to focus my time well. My accountability partner once shared that he'd rather work a sharp forty-hour week than a sloppy sixty-hour week. I have applied this truth to the parallel track journey and God has allowed me to make an impact in a variety of ways, bringing great joy and fulfillment.

INFLUENCING YOUR WORK . . . INTEGRATING YOUR FAITH

- What part of your Monday through Saturday life do you need to surrender to God?
- What biblical practices do you want to integrate into your work environment?

/////////////////

PAUL ANTHES *is president and founder of Financial Advisory Corporation and founder and lead coach of R3 Coaching. He holds the designations CFP® and CKA®. Activities outside of work include being a member of the board of trustees at Indiana Wesleyan University, board chair for the Ron Blue Institute at Indiana Wesleyan University, along with periodic speaking, teaching, and mentoring activities. Paul is married to Cindie and they have two children.*

4
GOD'S HUSTLER

DAMON THRASH

You intended to harm me, but God intended it all for good. He brought me to this position so I could save the lives of many people.
—Genesis 50:20 (NLT)

I grew up in Pensacola, Florida, which might seem like a beautiful beach area with a lot of military personnel. But I grew up in a drug-ridden, impoverished, and dangerous housing project in the early 1980s. My stepdad went to jail frequently for selling drugs, so for most of my childhood, my mom raised me and my three sisters as a single parent.

When I entered middle school, the crack era was starting to emerge. As a kid, I unconsciously watched every move of my stepdad and through him I learned things about the drug trade that others my age would have never known.

My mom was working her butt off to make sure that we had a roof over our heads, and I was in sports: basketball, baseball, and football. I would burn tons of calories all day and I'd come home with nothing to eat. That's when I started to really get that we were poor, and I decided to do something about it.

We moved to a different housing project that moved at a slower pace in the drug game and at eleven I already knew how to play the game. I was a pretty great student in school, but no one took interest in me or saw my potential, and in my hood, most of the black men were either abusing drugs or selling them. So, I started hustling before I was even a teenager.

There was a lot of money to be made in drugs, very quickly. It would typically be dangerous for a kid like me getting in the game, but I got a pass because I had family in the business. I could market my product and make money fast. By the time I was fourteen, I was making at least 500 dollars a day, even up to 2,000 dollars a day. I tried to hide this from my mom but eventually she picked up on it and kicked me out of the house for a time.

Some might think of this as a horrible story, but at the time I thought I had made it. Dealing took away poverty and the feeling like I wasn't in control. It took away school, which was easy for a bright kid, but annoying. I remember thinking, "Wow, this is a solution to pretty much every problem I have."

I started frequenting clubs with older guys. Because I could hustle, the older guys in the game who controlled the market wanted me on their team. It felt kind of like a bidding war for my talents—like a draft pick. I was sleeping in half of the day, hustling into the night, and buying anything I wanted, from expensive jewelry to designer clothes. Girls and even grown women wanted to be with me. I would send roses to a girl I liked in high school and it would be on. I would sell drugs and then use some of the money to buy Nintendo games or take a cab to go to the mall and pig out on fast food with my friends. It was a strange and exciting world for me, and I wasn't going to give it up.

A DANGEROUS GAME

Eventually a drug deal went south, and I ended up with a juvenile record and probation. When I got back to my hood after jail, it was as if I got a big coming-of-age celebration. I had passed the test. (This is especially true if you didn't snitch on anyone.) At that point, as sort of a rite of passage, I was introduced to using powder cocaine, and I liked it. I went through a spell of a couple of years using while selling drugs, and it almost killed me. I overdosed twice.

At one point, in order to hide my cocaine while a task force cop was chasing me, I ate my supply. I already had a bunch in my system, so this was super dangerous. When the task force realized I was clean, they let me go. My buddy quickly took me to buy a gallon of milk, which I chugged in order to make myself throw up. We thought I threw up all the cocaine, but I did not; I began to overdose. My whole body was reacting, vibrating insanely. A neighbor who was a nurse grabbed me from behind and attempted to eject all the foam from my stomach. I ended up in the hospital and was under for about two days. I remember having cotton balls taped over my eyes because they wouldn't close as I came out of the cocaine coma. It was like a dream. I eventually snuck out of the hospital.

After a second overdose I stopped doing blow. I discovered that, in reality, my biggest addiction wasn't cocaine or alcohol, it was control and the feeling of making fast money. I loved the power and the hustle and bustle of enterprise.

I was very successful, starting much earlier and lasting longer than anybody else. But almost everyone in the game expects it to end eventually. Either you die or you go to state or federal prison for major prison numbers (terms of sentence). The hope is to stretch it out and live for today as long as possible. I did it for a little more than a decade.

Running like I did means you become a top prize for law enforcement. Eventually they came and bagged me, pulling me in secretly to try to get me to talk instead of a big public bust. This was not a surprise to me at all, so I tried to play the situation. I figured I was going away for some stretch of prison numbers, so I needed to get my affairs in order. This worked until they figured out what I was doing, then they dropped the hammer and prosecuted me. I was sentenced to twenty years in prison for conspiracy to traffic up to 150 kilos of cocaine.

You might think that my life would finally turn around at that point. After looking down the barrel of twenty years, you'd think I would feel the weight of my actions and realize I was on the wrong track.

Nope. That's rarely how it works, especially for someone in the hustling world. For some people higher up in this business, prison doesn't break you; it makes you. The prisoners rolled out the red carpet for me. I was a shot caller on the street, so I was a shot caller from day one in prison. This was especially true since I kept my mouth shut and didn't give up anyone. (The first people who greet you when you enter prison are your homeboys; these are the hustlers who are from the city, state, or region you are from. I knew a bunch of people in prison; some were already in my extended drug business network.)

> *I'm hustling with a purpose now. I get up every day to make sure that somebody knows that they have these gifts and God can use them to do a good and great thing through entrepreneurship and enterprise.*

//////////////////

Was it different? Yes. But the dangers and the benefits of the streets are the same in prison; they are just more compact due to the close quarters. Turns out my whole life hustling on the streets groomed me for running my business in prison.

Others with a twenty-year sentence would expect to do seventeen or eighteen years. I was optimistic about my appeal, but figured I would do the full twenty because of my continued criminal enterprise. People will testify that even while you are in prison, you can still control the business on the streets. That's how it is. To me, it's not very different than some billionaire living in Europe while conducting their business in the United States.

TURNING POINT

While I was in prison, one of my closest friends was killed in Arizona. It really tore me up because I talked to him the night before. He was one of the guys on the inside that I groomed in the business on how to make money when he got outside. He did really well when he got out. We talked every day. But

//////////////////////////

then he was murdered. A few days later, I got thrown in the hole (solitary confinement)—which was not that unusual—but I was already hurting because of my friend's murder.

A chaplain came to visit me in the hole, the only one who's allowed, and gave me more terrible news; my mom was in the ICU at the hospital. She had been diagnosed with a really aggressive form of breast cancer and was undergoing a double mastectomy. I was blown away—just stunned—but still holding it together. After all of these years being addicted to the control of the business, I still believed I was controlling it all, even in that tiny cell where I couldn't even stretch out or talk to anyone for many days at a time. I still thought I had it all under my control.

The next day, I found out that my sister was diagnosed with an aggressive form of thyroid cancer. This time I started to lose it. I was in the hole for a week, just freaking out over all that was happening. I remember it was so very hot in the hole, I would sweat and sweat. It was all concrete, so I would take off all my clothes and lay with my full body on the concrete floor because it was cooler than the sweltering air of the room. I would lay there, trying to cool off, my tears mixing with the sweat on the sides of my head.

The lawyer came to tell me then that I'd lost my appeal. Now it was confirmed that I had thirteen more years to go on my sentence, and that very week I also found out that a huge amount of the money I had stashed outside was taken by someone I trusted and now it was gone.

I just broke down. I cried out to God in the hole. I was so overwhelmed I passed out. I slept and slept for days. It was so surreal. It was a new experience to sleep like that, in a place designed to not let you sleep comfortably. Some kind of new peace came over me, a kind of release. I learned later that this was the peace that is beyond understanding, as it says in Philippians 4:7 (NLT): "Then you will experience God's peace, which exceeds anything we can understand."

They finally woke me up by banging on the bars to get me to eat something. I prayed to God again, and again, and again. Then I noticed a book with no cover and disfigured pages under my bunk. I started reading it nonstop. I couldn't put it down. Time passed and before I knew it, I had read the Bible almost three times. When I was suddenly released from the hole and hit genpop (general population), I found out my mom and sister had pulled through and sent messages of love. A few weeks later they came to visit me. Everything started feeling so much lighter and I just turned around my focus. All my homeboys thought this new Damon was gonna last for only a couple of weeks. But it lasted from that point on all the way until this day.

What's amazing is I instantly had a clear sense of who God created me to be. I knew my limitations, but I also knew my purpose, gifts, and talents. I realized that God had given me this drive to be an entrepreneur and businessman, but I had only seen how to do it in the drug game. I realized that if I could establish a criminal enterprise on the streets and in prison, I could do a social enterprise effectively instead. I started a new business, but this one was to help other people who come from a similar background and community with a lack of legit opportunities to start businesses. Many are prisoners gifted with natural entrepreneurial skills like me and have learned these skills on the streets and in prison. So I started Divine Hustle Media, LLC, a social enterprise created to develop entrepreneurial transitional prep. I began writing a faith-based curriculum, called *Hustle Smarter*, while still in prison. I figured that if I waited until I was out, thirteen years later, I wouldn't do it. I would get out and get right back into the drug game.

Once the curriculum was drafted, I launched into the systems processes, marketing, and business plan. I created Inc. to Inc. (Incarcerated to Incorporated), a nonprofit that provides *Hustle Smarter* for free to anyone who can't afford it but wants to change their life and the lives of others through legal entrepreneurship. *Hustle Smarter* prepares people to be confident in their skills, talent, and purpose, and develop a business plan in prison and start launching it before they get out.

I went into prison two months before my twenty-third birthday. Others were just getting done with school and I already had my whole hustling career by then and I was "graduating" off to prison for half my life. I ended up getting out after seventeen years and eight months. I was forty-one. I grew up in prison and God changed my entire focus.

I'm hustling with a purpose now. I get up every day to make sure that somebody knows that they have these gifts and God can use them to do a good and great thing through entrepreneurship and enterprise.

One of my first success stories is Cedric. I helped him while we were both in prison. He saw me all the time sitting at a table with papers and books, making plans. He was curious and approached me. Day after day, he kept coming to my table so eventually I convinced him that if he sat with me and did the work, he could launch a successful business when he got out . . . and he did.

Cedric launched a business called Text to Write. It's a messaging application that allows military families and the families of the incarcerated to text a letter by logging into a mobile app. It automates the letter-writing process by eliminating the need for a pen, paper, and a stamped envelope, and sends it to the person who is in prison. That is some ingenious stuff he figured out how to do. He's doing well with that and other businesses now that he's out of prison.

As this happens, and as these lives are turned around and communities are redeemed, it is like God is flipping the evil plan of the Enemy on its head. Many people like me can now say, along with Joseph in the Bible, "You intended to harm me, but God intended it for good. He brought me to this position so I could save the lives of many people" (Gen. 50:20 NLT). Lives are saved when we take the evil intent of the Enemy and turn it into meaningful businesses like these.

I have found that many of the skills and ingenuity that it takes to run a criminal enterprise are the same that are needed for a legit entrepreneur. Once people figure this out, it's transformative for their lives. They commit to transform their hustle into hustling for God for good. We've realized that hustle is God's divine gift in these entrepreneurs.

INFLUENCING YOUR WORK . . . INTEGRATING YOUR FAITH

- What is something in your life that the Enemy meant for evil that can now be used for good?
- What could you take the initiative on now and hustle to make possible, instead of waiting on circumstances to change?

DAMON THRASH is the founder of Inc. to Inc. Entresition Services. After serving seventeen years in prison, Damon now provides personal and professional development opportunities to nonviolent offenders as an alternative to incarceration and paths to successful reentry into society.

5
A LIFETIME OF QUALITY CARE

GARY OTT

> *So do not fear, for I am with you;*
> *do not be dismayed, for I am your God.*
> *I will strengthen you and help you;*
> *I will uphold you with my righteous right hand.*
> —Isaiah 41:10

I've been the president of TLC Management since 1987. We manage twenty nursing homes in Indiana and Florida, and the company has grown steadily to the point that we have fifty companies to run and manage, along with 3,000 employees. However, to make sense of what my life is like now, I first need to tell you about my journey to become a business leader.

I grew up in the church and was baptized in the sixth grade, but the problem was that it was not my idea, it was my mom's. She said, "You and your brother will be baptized today." I went to church and attended a Christian school all because of my parents. They saw to it that I did certain things. But in the end, it was not really my faith, and something had to shift in me to make it my own.

While I was in college, I hitchhiked to Explo '72, a big Billy Graham crusade and concert event in Dallas, Texas. A friend of mine was going from Oklahoma and I told him I'd meet him there. I hitchhiked from Indiana to Texas, but I wasn't going for religious reasons; I was just going to have fun with a friend. But when I got there, something happened in that crusade that just ripped me apart. I realized I was still lost, even though I had all this Christian upbringing, and I made a faith decision right there at the stadium.

My life prior to that in college was not a good example of the Christian life, but by the time I hitchhiked back to Indiana, I was a changed guy. Everyone could see that I was different.

SEEKING STABILITY, FINDING FAITH

After that, I went into the military and even though my faith was finally my own, it was very difficult for me to be a Christian in that environment. I think the old-timers would have said I was "backsliding" at that point. Then the best thing that happened to me was getting to marry to my college sweetheart, Connie. I left the military after eight years because they wanted to deploy me again and I needed to have a more stable life.

I worked in Texas for many years after that and it was hard because we were a young family and were not making that much money. During that time, my mom was dying and it was really hard to be away from my family. I went back to Indiana for the funeral and decided to move back to be closer to the family and my dad. I got what I thought would be a lifelong dream job as a pilot, which is what I did in the military. I thought it was all coming together but the company went bankrupt and lost the plane I was flying for them. When I asked them about it, wondering what I would fly, they said, "Oh yeah, this is your last day." So there went that!

I remember being really upset with God because I just wanted a job so I could provide for my growing family. The only thing that was open was a management position in a nursing home. That is something I never thought I would do. I couldn't stand the idea of working in the medical field and being in a nursing home. So even though I was desperate, I turned down that opportunity. I remember going to an interview for what I thought was a management job, so I showed up in my suit and tie with a briefcase, but found out it was a carpet cleaning job. You could say I was not only overqualified but very, very overdressed.

I ended up driving around the downtown of my city with the plan to keep driving until I either found a job or ran out of gas. I had a huge burden and I couldn't eat or sleep well. I remember telling God, "I will do *anything*." Then, I remembered about that nursing home job. I said to God, "Fine, I'll do anything; I'll even work in a nursing home."

So I got that job and decided I would try my best to have fun and enjoy it. Well, it turned out that I fell in love with elderly people who were in their twilight years. I realized that working with them made me feel good. That had never happened to me in any job I'd ever had in my life. I did the job well and we were successful.

At some point, the owner decided he wanted to sell the business. I was interested but I didn't have the money. I got connected with other businessmen, brothers Larry and John Maxwell, who became my partners and financial backers. It was such a blessing to have these godly men become my mentors and help me start this new business. I recruited a strong team around me, including my own brothers who each had specific skill sets to really help us grow and become a solid business.

THE BOTTOMLESS PIT

In the middle of all this, after one of the most successful years of business, I decided to take my family skiing. Out on the mountain, I had an accident where I fell on my ski pole. Because of that I had to get a CT scan, and they rushed me in for emergency surgery. They said I had massive fluid in my abdomen. They didn't know what it was, but they believed I had ruptured something. After the surgery, I came out thinking that it was just a cracked rib but the doctor said it was much worse. He told me they found a tumor, and it was cancer, and it was all over the place.

I felt like I was falling into a bottomless pit at that moment. I didn't understand why this was happening to me and I didn't want anyone to see me in this very depressed state of mind. People wanted to come and pray with me, but I didn't want to have them. I finally relented when my wife pressed me, but my heart wasn't in it. I figured it might be doing something for them to come and anoint me with oil, but I didn't think much of it.

In this journey of God bringing me to my knees, I realized that I was not in control of anything, even though I had all this worldly success. The doctor basically said that if I didn't do anything, I had a zero chance of living. If I did chemotherapy, then it was 25 percent, but if I did chemotherapy and surgery, then I would have about 60 percent chance of living. So I told him I would do chemo and surgery.

I had to wait three months to heal from the first surgery. It was difficult for me—since I'm not a patient person—to wait upon the Lord's answer. During that time, Isaiah 41:10 was my rock. It says, "So do not fear, for I am with you; do not be dismayed, for I am your God. I will strengthen you and help you; I will uphold you with my righteous right hand."

I was anointed with oil for healing and several saints from my church prayed for me. After the chemo and surgery, I was completely healed from cancer and have been healthy since.

After that experience, I had a real shift in my outlook. I now know that there is a difference between my job and my work. My job is to be the CEO and president of a company that employs all these people and does all this key work. But my *work* is the vocation of caring for other people's parents as if they were my parents. In that work, I am trying to instill this ideal into our culture, where every doctor, nurse, janitor, or administrator is striving toward the same goal. I want us all to be shaped with that understanding so that when we hold hands with someone who is about to meet eternity, we treat them like they are our own parents.

MAKING THE MOST OF EVERY OPPORTUNITY

I want to be a witness to what God has done to me, in whatever way I can while I am building these relationships and building this culture. Sometimes it's just through a private and simple conversation, and other times it is a surprise. One time, I had flown with my insurance agent somewhere and when we returned, I couldn't get the landing gear to go down—which is a big problem. We ending up flying over Marion, Indiana, for two hours, trying to navigate the gear. As we were doing this—and getting really nervous—I figured I had better share my faith with him in more detail. So I shared the gospel while attempting to get the landing gear down.

It turned out that the insurance agent was already a believer, but I just wanted to be sure. We never did get the landing gear down and had to land on the belly of the plane—which is really dangerous—but God protected us. I recalled the incident to my pastor later and realized that you might say the agent was a bit of a captive audience. I promised I hadn't done it on purpose!

Another transforming event for me started at a hardware store. I was picking something up quick and I was going to be

In this journey of God bringing me to my knees, I realized that I was not in control of anything, even though I had all this worldly success.

late to see one of my grandkids play soccer. Within two to three minutes, I got what I needed and ran to check out. I didn't have time to mess around.

Once I got to the counter somebody behind me said, "Gary, have you got a minute?" Before even turning around I said, "No, actually I'm in a hurry. I'm trying to get to a soccer game for my grandkid."

When I finally turned around, I recognized the guy and his face fell as he blurted out, "Well, I just wanted to tell you I just found out I got cancer."

Now, I'm not as good at showing compassion to people as my wife is, but this guy's news blew me away and I invited him over to my house that evening. He came with his wife to spend time with us.

I told him my cancer story and he listened to it all and was taken by the spiritual story I was telling. He said, "I need Christ in my life. Can you get me Christ?" I figured it was time to pray together, so we went to another room to pray. At the end of the prayer I asked him how he felt. He replied, "I didn't get it. God didn't come in my life. I didn't get it."

This was new to me. I had no idea what was going on and I was a little stunned and unsure how to answer. After thinking a moment, I felt that God gave me insight to ask him a question. I asked, "Well, are you willing to pray for God to be in your heart and follow Jesus even if God doesn't heal you of the cancer?"

My friend answered, "Yes, I want God, whatever happens." So we prayed again and with all his heart he said, "God, I want you in my life and I'm willing to pray this prayer no matter if you cure me or not."

As we were getting to the end of his prayer, his phone started to ring. We ignored it—I mean, this was a key conversation and a key prayer. It rang again and we both tried to ignore it. Eventually it rang again and I told him, "You know, you should answer that. Maybe one of your kids is trying to reach you and is worried."

He picked up the phone and it was his doctor. The doctor said he was trying to get ahold of him because his additional tests had come back and showed that the cancer was isolated and would be able to be removed without any complications.

He hung up the phone and praised God. We didn't fully understand what was going on. He had the test done before we even met and before he even prayed. Healing was not a part of his prayer, but my friend wanted God just for God, and God wanted to heal him even if he didn't ask for it.

I think in my life I always thought of pastors, ministers, and missionaries as the ones that were responsible for evangelism and discipleship, but the influence of the Maxwells helped me rethink that. I have learned that I need to mentor people in the way of God within their sphere of influence and life context. It's not just a pastor's job but the work of all disciples of Christ.

- What is the difference between your job and your work?
- Who can you influence around you with just a listening ear?

GARY OTT *is the president and CEO of TLC Management, Inc., a provider of health and rehabilitation centers, assisted living and retirement centers, and hospice services. Gary and his wife, Connie, married in 1975 and have three children.*

6
THE GIFT OF LIVING
THE GREAT COMMISSION

BEN PAULSEN

> *In the same way, let your light shine before others, that they may*
> *see your good deeds and glorify your Father in heaven.*
> —Matthew 5:16

I was one of those kids who had grown up around church and prayed to "accept Jesus" probably a hundred times, but it never really was the main thing in my life. The most important things in my life were baseball, football, basketball, and being popular.

Things shifted when I went to work at a Christian camp. It was the first time I saw young people my own age who really loved God. I could see just by looking in their eyes that to them, God was real. They lived every minute this way and you could see it by the way they loved each other. At one point I remember thinking to myself, "Wait a minute . . . what if God really is real?" At that moment, it all came crashing into my soul and I just fell in love with God. My whole life turned around that summer and I would have run down the hill at full speed, just to spend time with God.

MD

I'm sure I had heard the verse before, but after that life-changing experience, I had new ears for Matthew 28:18–20. When I heard those words, they sounded like marching orders, as if I was hearing them for the first time. I heard Jesus say, "all authority," "heaven and earth," and then, "Go and make disciples of all nations." I just kept thinking and thinking about it. I felt like God was telling me, "That's for you." I was so excited. I knew what I was supposed to do with my life.

My dad was supportive of my awakening, but he stressed to me that I needed to go get a practical skill in college and not jump right into what I felt called to. I was discouraged because I thought I should go somewhere right away. I felt like Jesus would come back right at that moment and I would be wasting time.

But at my dad's request, I went to school. I was in what some called an "exploratory major," which was another way of saying "undecided," and that embarrassed me when people would ask what my major was. One day, I went into the woods during a huge storm. God put 1 John 3:18 on my heart, which says, "Dear children, let us not love with words or speech but with actions and in truth." As clearly as I've ever heard God speak, I sensed these words: "I want you to be a doctor." God wanted me to care for people with actions and in truth and use medicine as a bridge of friendship, which I could then use to tell people about God in a country where other Christians couldn't.

THE FIRST GRAVE

Moving forward with my story, there are three graves that greatly influenced the direction of my life.

In my twenties I was married to my wonderful wife, Brenda, and working as a doctor in a small town of 5,000 people, with a total of 10,000 in the whole county. The state paid for my education if I promised to work for a season as a doctor in a small rural town and I was doing a good job practicing medicine in an area that needed local physicians.

One day, I was on a flight and there was a moment when the plane lurched down in the air for a minute. Looking back on it, it might seem silly, but perhaps you have felt like me—your life seems like it might end, right then and there, like something from a movie.

The first thought that came into my mind was one I'm embarrassed to admit. Being a doctor in America, you can make a lot of money and my first thought was, "Oh, no, all that money I put into stocks. It's all for nothing, all useless."

Of course, the plane steadied after maybe 2.7 seconds or something and I felt such great remorse and self-loathing. Why in the world would that be the first thought that came to my mind? It woke me up to how off-course I had gotten. God wanted me to become a doctor so I could go somewhere others couldn't, and offer them first, physical healing, and second, spiritual healing in our Father in heaven.

Part of why I had gotten off track was that I felt the call to go, but my wife wasn't sure we were supposed to do long-term missions and wondered if we might just be able to do short-term missions and live in the States. That's a big deal. I would go by the cemetery in our town and think, "That's where my grave is gonna be."

I loved working in that town. The people were amazing. We had a comfortable financial life and already had a small family. It was ideal. It was a great life. But in my heart, I knew that was not my destiny. There shouldn't be a grave in that place for me. I knew it, but I couldn't see how it would change so I just suppressed it and chugged along, doing what I needed to do.

We were going to build a new clinic in our town, and I met with an architect to plan the building. Six months went by, and we were moving pretty far along the path. I found some land and I was about to put 12,500 dollars down on the land as a down payment. I got home that night and my wife asked, "Ben, did you buy that land today?" I said, "No, the guy went out of town. He's going to come back on Monday and I'm going to put the down payment on it then."

That's when she revealed to me that for the past six months she had been sensing from God that she should soften her view of us living as long-term missionaries. I was

stunned. God was working on her the whole time I had given it over to him and was feeling this heartache. That's how we ended up in Central Asia in the 1990s with our three kids.

THE SECOND GRAVE

I remember the hardest moment was after we were in Central Asia for a time and we didn't speak the language. I couldn't practice medicine yet because I was in language study. We were trying to build a hospital unit for orphans, but it wasn't going well.

My wife was expecting our fourth child and had some complications near the eleventh week of pregnancy. We got an ultrasound and the heart was beating, but they couldn't see the baby very well, so we had another ultrasound a month later. The baby was diagnosed as anencephalic, which means that the head was not closed. At first, I didn't understand the word in their language but when I finally understood I was so broken. I thought, "God! We gave up everything to follow you to this country, how could this be? How could you take this child from us?"

I'm so grateful because, at that moment, I felt like he spoke directly to my heart, "Ben, I am here." It was the most amazing experience. There in my darkest moment, I felt as if I were in an ocean of God's presence. It was just above my head separated by a very thin sheet—like crepe paper—and all I had to do was reach up and touch it and this ocean would just pour down and flow upon me. So I did that, I reached up and I felt his presence was real, tangible, touchable, feel-able, like solid grace just pouring all over me, even though we had just found out that our daughter would never live outside the womb.

People told us that since there was no chance that the baby could survive after birth, we should just abort her; that was never a consideration for us. Brenda could feel the baby move even though she had very weak kicks. Finally, the labor came and about five minutes before Anna was born, her heart stopped beating. We buried Anna in our adopted country and on the back of the tombstone, in English and our new language, we have the words "a seed planted remembered by many." That was inspired by John 12:24, where Jesus said, "Very truly I tell you, unless a kernel of wheat falls to the ground and dies, it remains only a single seed. But if it dies, it produces many seeds." I still don't understand why my daughter died, but we prayed for her to be a seed planted, producing many.

Not long after my daughter died, I had another moment in a plane where, for just a few seconds, it felt like it might go down. It was an interesting moment, almost like a funny test from God. This time, I wasn't embarrassed by my first thoughts. Instead, I was flooded with great joy in my heart, because when I die, I know I'm going to see Jesus and see the daughter we lost.

Out of that season, things slowly and surely began to mature and connect. Eventually we began to provide excellent patient care and practice letting our light shine, like in Matthew 5:16: "In the same way, let your light shine before others, that they may see your good deeds and glorify your Father in heaven." For that purpose, we work in orphanages, village clinics, nursing homes, do HIV work, disaster relief, train doctors, and do work overseas and in neighboring countries.

Sometimes people see the good work. They see light, but they don't know why. Sometimes we have to open our mouths and explain that it isn't because we're good people. It is because of Jesus Christ in our lives. As we do that and people come to know God, we teach them to obey everything that he's commanded, living out the Great Commission quite literally. We start groups of people who worship together, read the Bible, and become little churches. That is discipleship.

> *I reached up and I felt his presence was real, tangible, touchable, feel-able, like solid grace just pouring all over me, even though we had just found out that our daughter would never live outside the womb.*

One time, we were working on a little boy that was very ill. We worked hard and raised funds to get the surgery he needed, which was very difficult. His mother was a private Christian, but her family and friends were now mocking her because, to them, she believed in this mythology of Jesus and now she was going to lose her son.

But we were all praying and working. He was in the hospital for about a month and we were all in there praying and reading Scripture together. The surgery was a great success and it was fascinating to see how the mother's heart changed completely after that. She became a fireball for her Father in heaven, and she went back to her friends and neighbors to say, "Look at what God has done." Because of her witness, a new church was planted in her hometown and another one in a neighboring town.

THE THIRD GRAVE

While we were serving in our adopted country through medicine, a major epidemic struck our area. The government was very concerned about how it was all happening, but they didn't want an outsider like me to be too involved. I wanted to help, and I had the skills to help, so I offered. They took me in to interview me and in the end, they made me sign a paper saying I was doing all this of my own decision and that I understood the risks. That was a key moment for me. When you move to another country for the good news, you think a little about the potential cost, but this time, I had to think about it seriously.

I was memorizing parts of the book of John and there is a key moment in the first chapter where it says, "The Word became flesh" (v. 14). God's Word, the Son, became flesh in a man, Jesus Christ. I sure hope I have put flesh on the good news here, to actually be present, even in a risky season of epidemic.

Sometimes I wonder where my grave will be when I die. I wouldn't want my body to be shipped back to my country of origin. I remember visiting South Korea and going through a graveyard of some missionaries from the 1800s. They were buried right there among the people they came to serve and reach.

Like those missionaries from many years ago, I realize that this place has become my country. It would be pretty special for me to be buried here, near my precious daughter who died. I would be just another seed, planted for many. Why not? That's all any of us can ever hope to be.

INFLUENCING YOUR WORK ... INTEGRATING YOUR FAITH

- What do you need to leave behind in order to move toward the fullness of life God has for you?
- How might God be calling you to a hard place or a faraway place with your career as a tool for his glory?

DR. BEN PAULSEN and his wife moved to Central Asia in 1997 with three children and have lived there ever since. They now have nine children, some born in the family, some adopted or fostered, and one in heaven.

7
GOING PRO
FOR A PURPOSE

EVAN MAXWELL

> *I . . . urge you to walk in a manner worthy of the calling to which you have been called.*
> —Ephesians 4:1(ESV)

As you might imagine, being nearly seven feet tall makes me stand out in a crowd, but now that I'm a professional basketball player in Eastern Europe, my height doesn't make me stand out much at all. It's expected to have tall people in a pro ball locker room. What makes you stand out in professional basketball is the way you treat people. That is where I focus so much of my energy today—treating people differently. But that's not where things started out.

My family didn't push sports on me as a child. My dad was a drama director, worship leader, and professor. My mom played sports when she was younger, but I knew her as a stay-at-home mom, not as an athlete. Growing up, I was more into music and art. I played the guitar and served on the worship team. The dream in my head was to use these artistic things as a way to be in the world and be passionate about something.

By eighth grade, I was already six feet and five inches. My brothers were tall as well and they played basketball, so everyone at school was pushing me to play. I was terrible at first, but I was tall enough to make a difference. I made some of my best friends at the park playing pickup games every day.

As a freshman in high school, I made a huge jump in my game because I put in some hard work. I remember thinking, "I'm a hooper now." A traveling AAU team (Amateur Athletic Union) recruited me after a big game as a freshman. That coach picked me, gave me a scholarship, and put me in a weight training program. He asked me to commit six months of my life to it and told me that if I did, it would be life changing.

It was. I played there all through high school and that coach changed my life. He developed me as a person, helping turn the jerk of a kid I was into a man. I had a Division 1 NCAA basketball scholarship before my senior year of high school.

Even though I had a tug on my heart to live for God, I mostly just followed my flesh. On the court I fed my pride, which was contradictory to who I really was at my core. Instead of playing for a bigger purpose, it was all pride driven.

Growing up I went to Sunday school and I learned the right answers to religious questions. I basically did the right things and I acted like a good person, but I didn't own it personally. Once basketball began to consume my life, my faith went out the window.

It was as if I kept postponing my beliefs. In high school I thought: "When I get to college, I'll be a good full-time Christian."

When I got to college it was, "Well, when I am done with college ball I'll grow up and be a real Christian then." Eventually I had to stop postponing and figure out who I was. I consciously decided to take a step up the spiritual staircase, an endless journey that I've tripped and fallen over many times, but I continue to look up and keep climbing.

CALLED FOR A PURPOSE

My time in college at Liberty University and Indiana Wesleyan University shaped me to really take my faith seriously. My coaches truly cared about me outside of basketball, and they poured into my life. I started to be the person I wanted to become. I didn't want to return to the patterns and habits that pulled me down. Instead of just trying to win on the court, I started to try to win with my faith.

Ephesians 4:1–3 became a big part of my life. It says, "I . . . urge you to walk in a manner worthy of the calling to which you have been called, with all humility and gentleness, with patience, bearing with one another in love, eager to maintain the unity of the Spirit in the bond of peace" (ESV).

I began to choose to "walk in a manner worthy of the calling" (v. 1). At first, I didn't know what my calling was, but I wanted to find out and I wanted to fulfill whatever it would be. Now that I'm twenty-three and a full-time pro basketball player, I believe the main calling of my life is as a husband and a father. (My wife and child are with me in Slovakia.) I know God put in me from an early age a desire to be a good husband and father, so that is the core of who I am, even more than basketball.

Of course, God has led me to basketball, and he is using it. I have to be the best basketball player I can be, and I have to find a way to be like Jesus, no matter what my context is. My calling is not attached to my profession. My calling is being like Jesus. God first, others second, and I am third.

Playing professionally is a different ball game than college. There is none of the rah-rah and pray-together stuff I saw in college in the professional game. When I started playing professionally I thought the only way to make it was for me to be selfish, to get ahead individually, and not put others first. That is the temptation I face, but if I play like that, I don't like the game anymore.

I learned that if I put myself first and pursue basketball for me, I get depressed over time. Instead, the reason I play is about other people. I want to unite people because we can love the game together.

It is easy to say that I am third, but you skip over the most important part; "I am third" starts with putting God first. I intentionally choose things that influence me to make the right decisions throughout my day—things like listening to music that helps me think about Christ and reading the Bible.

The motivation needs to be clear in the end; it truly means all the glory goes to God. It's not about me—it's 100 percent about God. Putting others before yourself is what Jesus did and how he lived.

INFLUENCING PEOPLE FOR GOD

Now that I live in a new country, I'm getting used to it and it is starting to feel like home. I go out into the market and forget that people speak another language and it can be so hard to communicate. But I feel called to do what I'm doing right now, if for no other reason than to influence people for God. I know that God wants me to have influence, but God will strip it all away if I make it about myself and not about him. I'm blessed that right now I get to play a game for a job—a game that I love. I'm blessed that it comes naturally to me.

Interestingly enough, at one point in my life I felt like I was called to work overseas as a missionary, but that didn't make sense to me at the time at all. I didn't see myself as a missionary and didn't think I would want to live cross-culturally, so I pursued basketball and it took over much of my life.

But of course, you know what eventually happened. God now has me in another culture. He has a way of getting things done that don't make sense at the beginning, but it's always best to trust his plan. God doesn't make mistakes but uses broken people to do extraordinary things. I didn't see this life beforehand and wouldn't have chosen it originally, but if my main calling is to Christ, and he is first in my life, then wherever I am I need to respond to that calling. It helps to realize that *today* is my calling, not the future.

I have been playing basketball for ten years and for the last five years I've been trying to figure out how to fit God into the game. When God is not in my game, I become an ugly guy. If I play without him, I'm not myself. Pride and self-ishness come out when God is not first, and I have to find a way to incorporate God in how I play.

All that matters in the end is leading people to Christ. If I'm friends with someone for a long time and never bring up God, then what am I doing? God's given me size and abil-ities to have influence and relationships. Without prayer, opportunities might come up to talk about God, but I may not notice them happening. God might move, but I'm not a part of it. However, when I pray for God to open the doors for conversations, they happen.

PRAYING FOR OPEN DOORS

I have noticed that my spiritual impact has so much to do with my intentionality. I have found that I have to be intentional about my thoughts, praying that not only would God open doors, but that I would have the courage to walk through them. Since I have started praying that way, God has opened some of those doors already. There is one Slovakian I have been intentionally reaching out to. He is a super nice guy, but he isn't religious and doesn't believe in God. We went to lunch and just began the conversation of faith, God, afterlife, and relationship versus religion. It was really cool. He is a smart guy and has a really bad taste in his mouth about Christians, but he is open to talking and learning. Since that lunch, the door was opened for more conversations like that with him.

I consciously decided to take a step up the spiritual staircase, an endless journey that I've tripped and fallen over many times, but I continue to look up and keep climbing.

//////////////////////

It is hard to love people in this aggressive sport. Most think they play their best if they are angry or talk trash. Players will degrade each other and it's not personal, they just want to play better. God doesn't need that from me to be the best I can be. His work happens in love and grace even when I need to confront a player or be firm about my convictions. I try to be like Jesus in whatever setting I'm in.

For example, there may be a guy on another team who has been guarding me and all we do is play ball. If I do the right thing, even in just twenty minutes of physical contact, God may show them that something is different about me. They could look me up on Google and maybe there is an article about me that would point them to God. I know that seems far-fetched but, in my mind, I want to make the most of that twenty minutes to ensure that those I play with and against see that I'm living differently. If we're at the free throw line and about to box each other out, I try to say something positive that builds respect. I believe that it makes a difference.

On my team, I have opportunities every day to exemplify Christ in what I do, spending extra time building relationships and saying things that help my teammates. They see me at my best and worst. If I act like a hypocrite, then my witness

//////////////////////////////////

is damaged, and I have to be authentic in order to dig out of that hole and come back from being a bad example.

All of this often starts with being intentional about praying for people and asking for openings to talk about God. If I truly want an impact, I must have conversations about faith, so I have to ask God for opportunities. At the end of the day, I have to ask God to multiply my small influence as I offer my best.

It is easy to doubt why God put me here and easy to feel alone and inadequate. But God has shown me how to be fearless because there is truly nothing to be afraid of. There is no failure because God takes care of it all. Even if I make mistakes, God flips it to be used for good.

INFLUENCING YOUR WORK . . . INTEGRATING YOUR FAITH

- How can the passions you pursue glorify God?
- What motivates you to "walk in a manner worthy of the calling" (Eph. 4:1 ESV) in your work?

EVAN MAXWELL, *his wife, and child live in Europe where he is a professional basketball player. The six-foot-ten power forward has played with BK Spisska Nova Ves of the Slovak Basketball League. He earned a spot as an NAIA All-American at Indiana Wesleyan University twice, including a National Association of Intercollegiate Athletics Division II national title in 2018. He was a student athlete at Liberty University, the University of Kansas, and Abington Heights High School.*

8
PRAY FOR THE UNEXPECTED

DIANE FOLEY

"For I know the plans I have for you," declares the Lord,
"plans to prosper you and not to harm you,
plans to give you hope and a future."
—Jeremiah 29:11

I grew up in Haiti on the mission field. My mom was a nurse, and I spent a lot of time at the hospital. I also translated for visiting medical teams, so I literally grew up around medicine. As a student, I was really good in science and math and it seemed like everyone who was good in science and math went to college to study pre-med, so I thought I would just do that.

I met a guy named Steve and we started dating. He was also pre-med, and because we got serious pretty quickly, I figured I would switch career paths because I didn't think two married people both being doctors would make sense. So I went to the college registrar to change my major to nursing. It just so happened that my father was serving as the registrar at that time, so that was a little intimidating to come to him with that decision in that way. In the meeting, my dad/registrar looked at me and said, "Diane, you know I think nursing is an amazing profession. That's not the point I want to speak to. Instead, I only have one question I'm going to ask you before I sign this paper: Have you prayed about this?"

That was a good question. I really hadn't at that point. It happened to be a week with special services happening at our college, and the speaker was talking about Jeremiah 29:11, "'For I know the plans I have for you,' declares the Lord, 'plans to prosper you and not to harm you, plans to give you hope and a future.'"

After the conversation with my dad, I attended the special services. I can't even remember the speaker's name, but I sensed clearly the Holy Spirit saying in my heart, "I've called you to be a doctor."

That was the first time that I really felt called into something, so I didn't switch my major. Later on, when I contemplated quitting during my residency and when I had a new baby, I heard another speaker talk on that exact same passage, and it reminded me of my calling and gave me the strength to continue.

I'm very glad I continued because it has given me the opportunity to work with families and help them parent their children in pediatrics. I was able to come alongside them, not only with medical things that were happening, but in all of the psychosocial things that happen during development and adolescence. Because of that work, I had the opportunity to share personal spiritual stories. In exam rooms and in conversations about physical challenges, I was able to place little hints about my faith, and if people pursued the conversation it gave me an open door to share.

Along the way, I had this presumption that my husband and I might go to the mission field with our medical experience, but that's not how it worked out. Instead, we've been intentional to take people on medical trips, even doctors who aren't believers. They just want to help people, so we take them along. We tell them up front that we are going in the name of Jesus and there will be devotionals they will be a part of, and if they're OK with that they are welcome to come. A man I'll call Dr. Martin had been on trips with us a few times, and his marriage had been on the rocks. As a result of those trips, our friendship with him, and serving together with a new perspective on life, Dr. Martin and his wife restored their relationship. Another time a nurse who went with us accepted Christ at one of our devotional times, and one time a girl went with us on a mission trip and later went back as an adult to be a teacher in Haiti.

Once, another doctor decided to go with us on a trip at the last minute near Christmas. It started to change his whole view of the world and now he's doing amazing things overseas to help people in a hundred ways. His whole life shifted in that direction. He's developed a nonprofit that is very active and has their own staff in Haiti, and he goes multiple times a year.

UNEXPECTED SHIFTS

After some changes and challenges in our practice, my husband and I ended up moving to Colorado and starting over, in many ways, professionally. That left me pursuing a position in a pregnancy resource center, something I had not expected. I focused on adolescent gynecology for teenage girls. The center had received a federal grant to teach abstinence-based sex education in Colorado Springs, and they needed somebody to coordinate that. So they asked me if I'd be willing to direct that program.

My first thought was, "No, I'm a doctor, I don't know anything about nonprofits." I was starting to decline the offer when the director said, "Well, would you be willing to pray about it?" That was the same phrase my dad had said to me so long ago. I did pray about it and God changed my mind, making it clear I should do it. That again changed the trajectory of my life.

By the time I left that work, we were working in seventeen high schools, with up to 7,000 teenagers impacted in what became a very successful program. At that point, I was approached by the executive director of Global Partners to work with the medical missionary cause around the world. This of course was close to my heart and after praying about it, I shifted to that work.

At the time, I presumed that this was what God had for us for the rest of our lives. It made perfect sense and I loved it.

The work was ramping up, and we were about to leave on a long medical mission trip to Haiti, but as we were boarding the plane, my phone rang. It was a friend from Health and Human Services in the US government, with whom I used to work with in another capacity. She would call me every now and then, asking me short medical questions and I would help quickly and move on. That's what I assumed it was, so I answered because I was planning to be off the grid for a long time.

If we can serve with integrity, regardless of position, and realize that the truth doesn't change based on circumstances, then we can influence the world for God.

She said, "Hey, did you read the paper this morning?" I hadn't. She told me that the deputy assistant secretary for the Office of Population Affairs had resigned the day before and they wanted me to submit my resume.

That was the easiest "No, thank you" I had ever given to anyone about an opening in my life. I mean, I love global work. I was a missionary. I was already living my calling, and it was perfectly wired up for me. I'm not a political person, and I'd never been an activist or a campaigner. I haven't been on a school board and I haven't worked on public policy. I voted in elections and prayed for my leaders, but that was about it. This was just too far off the radar for me to even consider. Besides, the logistics made no sense because my husband was locked in with his work in Colorado and this job was in Washington, DC. But then my friend said, "OK, but are you willing to pray about it?" So I left on our trip and we prayed about it while doing our medical mission work.

This was yet another time I dismissed something right away before I prayed about it. I've prayed about other things that God has not led me to, but after talking with God, it became clear I should put my name in. Well, I got appointed and I was off to Washington, DC.

BEING WISE WITH FAITH

The fear was creeping in . . . fear of what might be coming, fear of not being up to the task, and just general, total uncertainty. I kept thinking of Colossians 4:5–6, which says, "Be wise in the way you act toward outsiders; make the most of every opportunity. Let your conversation be always full of grace, seasoned with salt, so that you may know how to answer everyone." The other passage that instructed me so well was 1 Peter 3:15–16: "But in your hearts revere Christ as Lord. Always be prepared to give an answer to everyone who asks you to give the reason for the hope that you have. But do this with gentleness and respect, keeping a clear conscience, so that those who speak maliciously against your good behavior in Christ may be ashamed of their slander."

Now, our government is not a theocracy. I have to be wise with my faith. I am prepared to give an answer, but I'm not jockeying for position to insert my faith into every conversation.

In every sphere of our society we can have influence in this way. We must make the most of every opportunity, but not force opportunities where there are none. Many people get in a position of power or authority and they forget everything that brought them to that place. I think that's where Christians in the marketplace can make a difference. If we can serve with integrity, regardless of position, and realize that the truth doesn't change based on circumstances, then we can influence the world for God.

Discipleship definitely looks different now. In medicine, when you are teaching someone like an intern or resident, there are a lot of opportunities to display your integrity and to share what makes you tick. These apprenticeship moments are built into the world of being a doctor, and they can be a place where making disciples is more natural, since the teaching and sharing relationship is already baked into the arrangement of what you're both supposed to do.

However, in public policy and government, I've found that there's such a toxicity and aversion to many things, including faith. I want to be sure I present research on everything so that it is proven in a way that isn't swayed by faith alone. Certainly, the Constitution doesn't permit me to use my position to force faith on others. That is what separation of church and state means. However, that doesn't mean people of faith are not influenced by their faith while they work in government and public policy. I don't think we want a world where every decision we make is faithless.

It all matters so very much. The way we make these decisions can impact literally millions of people and of course, the way I treat those I work with matters, too. The same principles that apply to any other marketplace also apply to government work, it's just at a different level of responsibility and scope.

For me, it starts by not thinking of myself as better than others and being calm in the middle of what can feel like chaos. When that becomes the way I operate and how I build authentic relationships with people, then the redemptive conversations flow from there.

INFLUENCING YOUR WORK ... INTEGRATING YOUR FAITH

- How has a sense of fear stopped you from moving forward?
- How can you bring peace in the middle of a chaotic situation at work?

DR. DIANE FOLEY *serves as deputy assistant secretary for Population Affairs and director of the Office of Adolescent Health at the US Department of Health and Human Services (HHS) in Washington, DC. Dr. Foley spent most of her childhood in Haiti where her parents served as missionaries with The Wesleyan Church. She is a graduate of Marion College (now Indiana Wesleyan University) and of Indiana University School of Medicine. Her area of specialty is pediatrics with a focus on adolescent health as well as maternal and child health. She is married to Dr. Steven Foley and for over forty years they have shared the joys and struggles of ministry in the marketplace while raising four children. They now have three sons-in-law, a daughter-in-law and are the proud grandparents of ten amazing grandchildren.*

9
FAITH AND LOGIC

PHILIP FARRELL

Do your best to present yourself to God as one approved,
a worker who does not need to be ashamed and
who correctly handles the word of truth.
—2 Timothy 2:15

Growing up, we were the only black family of West Indian descent in a predominantly conservative Jewish Toronto neighbourhood. Naturally, you might say I stood out a bit given that no one at school had a black afro and almost everyone went to Schule on Saturday.

I remember a Jewish boy in grade four or five making fun of me because I had to go to church on Sunday.

I felt I had to defend the faith, so I went on and on saying, "You gotta accept Jesus to go to heaven or else you're going to hell!" The more he laughed, the more I cried. He continued to make fun of me and I'm pretty sure that left an indelible mark on my psyche and soul. I thought that talking publicly about your faith would leave you mocked and ridiculed (of course, that's exactly what Jesus went through too).

CALLING

I loved competitive sports, earning the Athlete of the Year trophy, Athlete of the School trophy, and a specially made trophy for me because I earned 2000 more points than any other athlete in the school. So at the time I was thinking that I was big stuff and that maybe basketball or high jump was in my future. But my Jewish gym teacher at my Jewish high school told me that I should become a doctor because it would benefit the black community. I was blown away by that, but I respected him and thought about his suggestion from that day forward.

Meanwhile at church, I was constantly told that I was called to be a minister of the gospel of Jesus Christ. In my last year of high school, I had people telling me I have to be a doctor and others telling me I needed to be a pastor and I had no idea what I was going to do with my life.

That summer I went to Silver Lake Wesleyan Camp, a youth camp in the Central Canada District. I asked God to help me work through this decision, and when all was said and done, engineering was the future for me, and God was calling me to minister in that world. It may sound strange, but I believe God called me to get a PhD and to "pastor" others that had the same analytical mindset.

I pursued three degrees in mechanical engineering and eventually was employed as a defence scientist (DS) for the Department of National Defence in Canada, where I ended up rubbing shoulders with science workers and administrators all day long. For eleven years in university and over twenty-eight years as a DS, I've likely had dozens of conversations about evolution and creation, how Christianity is different from "all the other fables and myths," and why there is so much evil in the world if God is so good. Thus, my calling to marketplace multiplication began.

> *. . . it is every Christian's calling to integrate those aspects of life that God believes are important, even in a scientific career like mine that might be considered intrinsically biased against faith-based practices.*

MARKETPLACE RESISTANCE

In my first year of university (that is, freshman year of college), our youth group went to a huge Wesleyan youth conference in Urbana, Illinois. They presented the opportunity for living a holy life and being sanctified. I made a commitment to holy living, which I took very seriously. At that time, I surrendered everything to the Lord, and he gave me his heart for people in the marketplace. It was fascinating because after that moment in my life, I began to have more opportunities to share my faith, including starting a

Bible study in the University of Toronto Mechanical Engineering Department, one of the most secular universities in the nation. The opportunities that emerged seemed almost endless. Even with the emotional scar I had from my childhood encounter with sharing my faith, I found that I was given the courage to talk with people about their spiritual lives.

However, there have been limits to how much I've been able to integrate my faith and my profession. In university, we had to write a paper on the social impact of technology. I chose to write a paper on what would happen in a developing country in terms of the social impact of technology. My mom, Beulah, and dad, Samuel, are from Nevis, West Indies, so I studied that island to see how they might interject love into the social settings of the technology sector. I found in my research of the Bible and other sources that people who loved God and their neighbour would often use technology for the benefit of society and not necessarily themselves. I thought it was a pretty fascinating project and that I had done excellent work. However, I got a C+ on that project even though I thought it was better than much of my other colleagues' work that received As. It got me thinking about whether I should ever try to interject Christian principles into scientific work. I was discouraged.

Over time, however, I came to believe that while there is some resistance and discrimination against Christian values, it is every Christian's calling to integrate those aspects of life that God believes are important, even in a scientific career like mine that might be considered intrinsically biased against faith-based practices.

God gave me an analytical mind and he clearly was preparing me to reach certain personalities that respond to logic and reasoning. However, leading with the "heaven and hell" argument that I'd unsuccessfully used as a child was probably not going to get me anywhere.

I realized I needed to read and understand the Bible cover-to-cover—much like I needed to read and understand my physics textbook inside and out. Studying the Bible would help me understand God's perspectives on the anticipated questions people would ask. This preparation has helped me tremendously as I reach people in my circle of influence that use logic to defend their beliefs.

FAITH IN THE SCIENTIFIC METHOD

A scientist starts with logic and observable data with which the null hypothesis is falsified (an often confusing "double negative" of sorts). One might hypothesize that if you eat apples you will surely die. The null hypothesis is that nothing happens when consuming apples.

Scientist A may easily prove the null hypothesis by introducing a time frame of, say, one hour after eating an apple. Although the percentage of people who die after eating an apple is nearly 0 percent, it is possible that people may die after eating an apple.

Scientist B may set the time frame to be 150 years and observe that 100 percent of individuals die within 150 years of eating the apple, thus falsifying the null hypothesis.

Food allergy is an immune system reaction that occurs soon after eating a certain food. Even a tiny amount of the allergy-causing food can trigger signs and symptoms such as digestive problems, hives or swollen airways. In some people, a food allergy can cause severe symptoms or even a life-threatening reaction known as anaphylaxis. Food allergy affects an estimated 6 to 8 percent of children under age 3 and up to 3 percent of adults. While there's no cure, some children outgrow their food allergy as they get older. Untreated, anaphylaxis [food allergy] can cause a coma or even death.[1]

Let's say both reports are submitted for publication and are peer reviewed. One report gets published and the other does not. For the published report, only two out of three reviewers recommend the report be published: how do we know that the two reviewers are wrong, and the single reviewer isn't right? The associate editor makes that judgment call, but how do we know that their judgment isn't impaired? The same questions could be asked of the report that didn't get published! Where's the objectivity, the "facts," the truth in all of this? And yet the peer review process is the basis for all science.

Even though I might not fully understand all the data and their implications in the papers that I read or produce, I still *trust* the process. I have *faith* that the scientific method can produce repeatable results for the betterment of humankind.

I *hope* that I have enough high-quality observations to prove or falsify the null hypothesis. I *believe* in the peer review process. That is, even science has faith-based practices. Nevertheless, our profession sometimes promotes science as fact, yet in fact, facts boil down to peer reviewed consensus and subjective opinions of (hopefully) repeatable phenomena the majority of the time.

SHARING FAITH

We could take a scientific approach and formulate a hypothesis related to God's existence, and then find evidence to falsify the null hypothesis (e.g., apologetics). But, for the vast majority of believers, God says to follow him (see Matt. 4:19) and be more like him (5:48) as a means of marketplace influence as a Christian. In my circles of influence, I've found this to be the most effective way of falsifying the null hypothesis and presenting Jesus than any of the scientific arguments that I had developed over the years.

Be that as it may, allow me to give you an example of one of those scientific, logical arguments. In my work, we study humans interacting with technology and how this impacts our cognition (perception, goal-setting, decision-making, communications, and behaviors). But there is a lot more involved in human-system interaction than just cognition. Humans display five fundamental aspects in who they are: physical, intellectual (cognition), emotional, relational, and spiritual. The spiritual aspect isn't a separate component as much as it encompasses and permeates all other aspects.

The area of study in psychology known as "human factors" has made excellent progress in the cognitive, physical, and social (relational) aspects of human work, some progress in terms of emotional aspects, and little if any progress on the spiritual component. That isn't to say that there is no work being done on the emotional and spiritual aspects in other fields, it's just not a focus area of human-systems interaction. Nevertheless, I believe it is a significant gap in our field of study.

When I presented this gap to my peers, I felt the tension rise in the room. They just did not want to go down that road, and I understand why. But more recently, there has been a surge in research to understand religion and even "ideologies" associated with several conflicts around the world and post-traumatic stress disorder (PTSD).

Although I've made little progress amongst my peers in gaining focus on how spirituality impacts human-systems interaction, it has started conversations that I never thought I would have. What I have found is that, after presenting these ideas, folks come to me privately and initiate a conversation about spiritual things, and sometimes that results in praying for them, which they might be publicly apprehensive about but privately appreciative.

REAL STORIES

A colleague and friend of mine named Ralph* was an atheist. He had no time for God and really pushed back on any spiritual conversations. After innumerable games of squash and badminton and one-on-one chats, his tone started to shift. It was clear he wasn't as resistant, and he even started spiritual conversations with me. It turns out that he had a great deal of spiritual oppression in his life. He shared this with me privately and his denial and resistance to God began to fade. He even joined a Bible study at our office.

Imagine that: an atheist showing up to study the Bible with science workers in a government facility! Long story short, he became a Christian and began to share his story with everyone in the building. Ralph shared it with such zeal that his supervisor came to me one day to ask what was going on with him and I was able to have a conversation with him about Ralph's journey.

Another opportunity came when I was traveling from Toronto to Calgary and booked my seat exactly twenty-four hours before departure so that I would have no one sitting beside me. This was important to me because the Spirit was convicting me of disobedience in my life and I simply didn't want to talk to anyone.

The plane was completely full, and a woman named Carmen* took up residence beside me with her mom. Our conversation started by exchanging occupations and eventually ended at an impasse.

When it was my turn to describe my job, I told her I was a human factors specialist and studied human-systems interaction. She asked what that meant and after offering an extended, well-rehearsed, somewhat prideful definition, I included in my reply, "The human comprises of five fundamental aspects: physical, intellectual, emotional, relational, and spiritual." She immediately picked up on the spiritual aspect and said, "I don't believe in the soul or spiritual realm or God."

So for more than two hours on this flight, an atheist, artist, and science teacher asked me many questions. The honest, frank, logical, very civil, and even intriguing conversation came down to Carmen asking, "So what you're saying, Dr. Phil, is that according to John 3:16, if someone doesn't believe in God then God will send them to hell even though they do good things?" And I responded as usual, "What I'm saying, Carmen, is that according to John 3:16, if someone does believe in God then God will welcome them into heaven even though they do good or bad things." The conversation stalled at this point with an eerie, stern, sad, confrontational, and unbelieving silence. We moved on to talk about the US primaries with another thirty minutes to go in the flight—much less controversial. (Smile.)

This time I didn't cry and Carmen didn't laugh at me, so I guess that's good. Nevertheless, I'm in good company with Jesus himself, who talked about heaven and hell plenty.

SOWING SEEDS

When it comes to sharing faith in a marketplace like mine, I am reminded of Matthew 13 and the sower of seed. Those who spread seed of the "good news" sow it in marketplaces where professional pastors and missionaries will never have an audience. Sometimes I feel like I'm planting just one seed in a few colleagues' lives over our entire careers together with little to no fruit. But over time, as the seed is planted in the soil of common work experiences and watered with encouragement and God's love, the seed begins to grow.

Jonah in the Bible was reluctant as well. He didn't want to stand up in Nineveh and tell them about God and how God viewed them. He didn't think the Ninevites were really worth it. I can feel like a Jonah at times. But God has shown me that if you're called and prepared and have the courage to share your faith, he will move in your workplace and sphere of influence.

Scripture is full of this message of hope. In John 10:10, Jesus tells us that he came to give life and life more abundantly. If you're like me and resisting because you're in a field that seems complacent, even hostile, towards Christianity, just think of Ralph, Carmen, and others who would not otherwise be exposed to God's love. Don't allow people's laughter to drown out Jesus' exciting call to share the good news.

Whatever field you're in, the Lord can take your personality and profession—if you're willing to offer them to him—and do marvelous works through you.

- What questions do people ask you in the workplace that give you the opportunity to share your faith?
- What is one thing you can do to prepare yourself to influence your coworkers?

DR. PHILIP S. E. FARRELL *works for Defence Research and Development in Canada as a defence scientist specializing in human factors research for CAF/DND. He has over 150 publications on various defence science and technology topics, served as DRDC's lead scientist, and is a former chair of the NATO Research Task Group Human Factors and Medicine Panel (HFM 252). He also sits on the boards of The Wesleyan Church and Kingswood University.*

*Names have been changed.
This chapter uses the Canadian spelling of select words.

NOTE
1. "Food Allergy," Mayo Clinic (website), accessed March 25, 2020, https://www.mayoclinic.org/diseases-conditions/food-allergy/symptoms-causes/syc-20355095.

10
ONE LIFE

YAREMÍ ALICEA-MORALES

But seek first his kingdom and his righteousness,
and all these things will be given to you as well.
—Matthew 6:33

My family and I are from Puerto Rico. There, I married my husband, Yamil, gave birth to our two kids, served in the church in different capacities, and started a rewarding professional career in the pharmaceutical industry. Little did I know that in 2015, at the brink of my fifteenth work anniversary, my career development would lead my family to The States. Although we knew that God was orchestrating the move, it was still very daunting, mainly because we left everyone we knew and loved—including a thriving ministry—back on the island and started over in the US. At first, I thought I would turn down that job opportunity, as good as it was, because it could be a lonely and uncertain thing to leave everyone and everything behind; but we strongly sensed that we needed to trust God in making the transition even when we didn't have all the answers to our questions. Within sixty days, we relocated to Indiana and found ourselves immersed in a new culture, environment, and language.

God has been faithful in unimaginable ways and has provided me with multiple opportunities, not only through growing professionally, but also to witness his favor. Although I have to be more careful in my professional setting, I can't live two lives, so I need to share my faith in my day-to-day life. Though I cannot share my faith overtly, that doesn't keep me from relating to others in a Jesus-loving way. The way I give back to people, the way that I coach people, and the way I put them first matters because it models the values of the kingdom of God within us. More specifically, regardless of the power-distance relationship—subordinates or colleagues—living a lifestyle that genuinely cares for others is what makes all the difference.

I don't always do this perfectly. There was a season in which I allowed my career to define my focus and passion—more precisely, my purpose. Then, I heard a sermon in church that helped me reframe my thinking. I realized again that my purpose was higher than my professional career. Moreover, my work and any success I could do alone did not give me purpose; I needed to bring God's purpose to my work. For this reason, I strive to do everything at work with utmost excellence because ultimately my boss is Jesus Christ. To him is my higher allegiance every step of the way in my career advancement.

LIVING ONE LIFE

I always have embraced my life as one. My faith is the whole me and my professional life is the whole me. If my faith is not a part of me at work, then am I really a person of faith? If I share with a coworker what is important to me in my life as we become friends, and faith is not a part of that, then is it truly important to me? Am I hiding something from that colleague for some reason? If I think about it, I might be failing in our friendship by not sharing something that is so vital to me. My work—professional skills and knowledge—needs to be a part of my faith too. I can't "turn on" my faith at church and "turn off" at work. Yes, I can take a Sabbath and choose not to do work, but because my career is part of who I am, the matters that are discussed at church should be applied in the workplace context as well. In the same way, I should not shy from sharing about my work experiences among my Christian relationships. All in all, God is at work in my whole life, therefore, I need to live an integrated life at all times.

God has given me opportunities to have kingdom-oriented conversations with people at work, and I have been able to start a group to read the Bible with other Christian believers. I prayed that God would make it clear who I should reach out to for regular meetings and two names came to my heart; I connected with them. I told them I was thinking of having a regular meeting to read and discuss Scripture right at work, and they were super happy and wanted to be a part of it. It was a surprise to find out that even though God brought those two women to my mind separately, they were actually friends with each other, and I didn't know that at all. God had prepared that in advance, and it helped our group connect with each other more quickly.

WORKING FOR A HIGHER PURPOSE

I have recently transitioned to a new role and I am thrilled with the potential opportunities this change will create to influence people through living my faith in an appropriate way; I know that I must use wisdom. Whenever there is a move or a change in leadership within a team, everyone enters into a period of acclimation. This could be a challenge, especially in the first few months of a new job. During that intro period, it is important to set the tone and deliver at the highest level. It is important to stay focused and trust that God is already at work long before my arrival to the team. What might be seen as a season of changes and adjustments is no more than opportunities to connect with new people, not merely as part of my professional growth, but because of my higher purpose as a follower of Jesus.

Almost twenty years ago while I was studying for ministry, a Christian colleague told me that my call was to those working in the business world. I took that to heart. I understood it as a confirmation of what God was already putting

. . . regardless of the power-distance relationship— subordinates or colleagues—living a lifestyle that genuinely cares for others is what makes all the difference.

//////////////////////

in my heart. Later, after I moved to the US, I went to a conference where someone prayed for me about my witnessing role in the business world, and it was a reconfirmation of what God had deposited in my heart a long time ago. I remember that this woman prayed for me that day saying, "God is anointing you for a job he is putting in your hands in the marketplace." That was something she couldn't have known the details to. She knew nothing about my new job or about me. God really blessed and helped reconfirm my calling, and anointed me for the career he was tailoring for me.

One of the biggest pieces of witnessing at work has been awareness of where the Holy Spirit is moving, and knowing when I should talk about my faith. Last year, I was in Europe for a work-related conference and met a woman whom I clicked with immediately. I was listening to her talk about her life and she began to ask me questions. I was open with her about the ways I live my faith as an individual and with my family. I could see that she was genuinely interested and wanted to continue the conversation further. This was someone that I didn't even know a week earlier, and in the span of just a few days, we were able to talk about matters of

//////////////////////////////

faith, life challenges, and the Bible. The turning point in the conversation was the moment I openly shared my life and Christian faith. We ended up praying and have stayed connected even after the conference. I am in awe to see how God has worked in her life since then.

My relationship with the Lord and my partnership in the kingdom of God helps clarify my purpose. He puts the desires in my heart for the right things. Once I have clarity on what I need to do, I just need to trust the Lord and act accordingly. It is critical to be sensitive to people and understand where they stand, but what is most important is to know what God is up to in the process. My role is to be faithful and obey, maintaining the pace, neither ahead, nor behind, but with God.

INFLUENCING YOUR WORK . . . INTEGRATING YOUR FAITH

- How can you practice faithful leadership in your workplace?
- Are you living two different lives, and if so, how can you bring them together?

YAREMÍ ALICEA-MORALES is a global marketing director and has eighteen-plus years of experience leading innovative brand strategy, global campaign development, and strategy execution within the US and global markets. Originally from Puerto Rico, Yaremí and her husband, Yamil, now live in Indiana with their two children.

11
DISCIPLESHIP IN EVERY OPPORTUNITY

JULIA PYLE

*Let us not be weary in doing good, for at the proper time
we will reap a harvest if we do not give up.*
—Galatians 6:9

I started my career working as a nurse in a faith-based organization, so my beliefs were an integral part of how my colleagues and I cared for patients. I was in the cardiac unit and then a critical care unit, and I often had opportunities to pray with people and share the gospel. In a faith-based institution, it was top of mind and out in the open.

Now I've been in a county-owned institution for more than a decade and the environment is such that I need to be more cautious about ideas that I share. It became a bigger challenge to integrate my faith and my work and, in some ways, I had to be more intentional. At the same time, I was adjusting to moving from a bedside role to an executive leadership role.

I began questioning myself, thinking, "I am living my faith outside my work. How can I integrate them better? How can I be a Christian and be an influence and further the kingdom where I'm at?"

JOURNEY TO LEADERSHIP

I started meeting with my pastor, Steve. We talked about what my purpose was and what my spiritual gifts were. Our church had just planted another church called Radiant Life. We were missing those we had sent to that new church and thinking about how we could lead our sending church forward. We read the book *The Executive Calling* by Roger Anderson together and that helped me find my voice in that journey. I embraced the idea that I am a leader, that I'm called to this role, and I'm also called to be a disciple-maker and live out my faith in the workplace. From then on, I looked for ways to use my position to be of influence and help grow and develop those under me. I wanted to have a biblical influence even if I wasn't directly quoting the Bible.

In my emergence as a leader, the story of Esther in the Bible greatly influenced me. She lived in a culture that was so ungodly and immoral. She could have easily doubted that she could do anything to bring about change, and then God used her in a mighty way. I began to think to myself, "Be an Esther, Julia!"

I grew up in a very legalistic faith tradition where women were to be silent and in the background. It's been a challenge to overcome those early impressions. Several years ago, I went to an Exponential church planting conference, and was greatly impacted to see what women were doing there. There was a powerful moment when they invited people to come forward to be anointed in their calling. I felt led to do so, even though it was way out of my comfort zone. When I came to the woman anointing people, she asked, "Are you a church planter?" I remember thinking, "No, I'm a disciple-maker." She anointed me in that moment saying, "The Holy Spirit is filling you with this laying on of hands." It felt like I was affirmed to do the work of disciple-making in the workplace.

For the first time, I began to see myself as a church leader and even like a pastor in some ways in my giftings, but that didn't mean I needed to quit my main job. I realized that I am where I am right now for a good reason, which gave me boldness and confidence in being a pastor in my position in the hospital.

I have several people that report to me directly whom I meet with one-on-one every month. We talk about what is going well and what isn't, and then share feedback for both

areas. This has started many in-depth conversations. I feel empowered to talk more about faith, which is easier to do with those whom I know have some faith or are church people already. Over time I am able to offer my biblical perspective in more ways.

When it comes to marketplace ministry, the application of the Word of God in my daily life is key. It's being mindful as to what God wants me to do in each situation. I'm vulnerable to ego and sometimes make decisions without stopping to pray, but I try to take the opportunity to consider God's heart as I make decisions, deal with management and peer supervision, and handle all the HR components of this job.

During a huge economic downturn, our hospital needed to cut positions and the hospital chaplain program was eliminated. I struggled with how to get this back into our work, but because we are a county-owned hospital it was tricky, even though there seemed to be wide support from employees.

The key here is that while I had a role as an individual, I also wanted to change the culture of my organization to be more receptive to spiritual conversations. I wanted to operationalize a new program focused on spiritual wellness without it being forced. A Christian nursing professor from a nearby university discussed this possibility with me and was really feeling conviction about it. God was moving in her life and she wanted to take the lead, so I supported her leadership.

After gathering early supporters in the organization, we launched a spiritual care committee, meeting internally with fifteen staff members in different zones, to develop a charter for intentionally launching a chaplain program. Patients and staff are offered a spiritual wellness "menu" to help them know what is available. A big part of why I'm passionate about this program is that it can be embedded in the structure and culture of the hospital beyond what I alone can do.

SPEAKING TRUTH INTO HARD SITUATIONS

Health care is difficult. I have to use my faith to overcome the stress of my role as a hospital administrator with more than 450 employees to oversee and lead. At any given moment, staff and managers are dealing with problems and crises. We have HR complaints, litigation, and other major issues coming to the forefront daily, at a high rate of speed. People pull on me from all directions and I have to center myself and survive it while attempting to thrive within it.

One example is when we have to let people go for infractions. We have to enforce policy internally and adhere to federal and state regulations, which sometimes results in people losing their jobs. Being able to show these employees—even at termination—grace and compassion is important.

One time a woman wanted to meet with me despite the fact that she was being let go. I think she somehow knew I had faith and simply needed to talk because she had some really pressing and hard things going on in her life. Holding her hand, I told her that I look to God for help through all hard situations and asked her if she wanted to pray together. She was crying and said yes, so I did. In other situations, people can be angry with me and don't want to hear from me, but I make the most of the opportunities I am given.

Other times I've found that forgiving an employee for something and showing them grace can make a big difference. I like to talk about forgiveness in this work, because we are all human and make mistakes. It is what we do when we make mistakes that matters. Just as Christ forgives me, I can do the same even with an employee whose faith I know nothing about. That is one way of integrating my faith in a practical way that makes a difference with others and improves the organization.

God can use the way I respond to people in these high-stress situations, so I don't underestimate his power. Love is important in leadership. Yes, we have to make people toe the line—accountability is important. But love isn't about ignoring problems. It's about speaking the truth in a loving way.

Lives are so messed up—I see broken bodies, broken families, and broken careers every day. Our women's life center is one area that reveals this brokenness. It mostly serves mothers who are in very difficult situations that are hard to imagine. Often, these women are parenting alone because the fathers are unknown or absent, or they're dealing with fights over custody of the children. These are real-life opportunities for God to show up. Christ always shows love, so anytime I interact with our employees and patients, I want to show love.

INTENTIONAL DISCIPLE-MAKING

This leadership growth in my life is having an influence beyond even my hospital and my local church. I am a part of a team from my church and several others that launched an organization called the Dirt Roads Network. This network is all about helping churches become river churches, not lake churches, meaning we want to multiply disciples and churches in a way that doesn't stay stagnant in one lake, but flows out like a river to many others through intentional discipleship.

I can live out my faith in disciple-making. I'm working with people most of the day so if I'm not making disciples at work, then where would I do that? All the things we talk about in church feed back into what I'm doing in the hospital, and living this way is part of what the Dirt Roads Network wants to spread. Multiplying the church means we need more people in jobs and fields like mine to take making disciples seriously; then the kingdom will grow, wherever we live and work.

When it comes to marketplace ministry, the application of the Word of God in my daily life is key.

In the process of all this learning, I was told that I have the giftings of an apostle. This blew my mind big time because of my background—women like me couldn't be ministers, much less have gifts like that. I went to an Alan Hirsch workshop and read his book *5Q: Reactivating the Original Intelligence and Capacity of the Body of Christ.* I learned about the apostle, prophet, evangelist, shepherd, and teacher giftings and how they work to equip the church to expand the kingdom of God.

The hero-maker message helped me understand how I don't need to be the hero; I need to make heroes out of others, letting them grow and make a difference. That's how I've come to deal with the ego side of people that some get caught up in. As leaders in the marketplace, we can be hero makers out of others. That isn't just good business; it's multiplying the kingdom of God.

INFLUENCING YOUR WORK ... INTEGRATING YOUR FAITH

- Is there a change you would like to make in your organization's culture?
- If so, what do you need to do to initiate that change?

JULIA PYLE, RN, MSN, is the chief operating officer at Newman Regional Health. Previously she served as chief nursing officer at Coffey Health System and intensive care and cardiac nurse at St. Luke's Hospital. Julia and her family live in Emporia, Kansas.

12
MINISTRY THROUGH FINANCE

PETE BENSON

> *Commit to the L*ord *whatever you do,*
> *and he will establish your plans.*
> —Proverbs 16:3

I grew up on the coast of Grand Manan Island in the Maritime provinces of Canada, east of Maine. My wife and I have been together forty-three years now. We grew up seven houses apart and have known each other since nursery school.

We went to Kingswood University, which at the time was Bethany Bible College, and I wasn't sure what I wanted to do with my life. My dad and grandfathers on both sides were entrepreneurs, and I always had a kind of independent entrepreneurial spirit. When I was in college, the idea of planting churches stood out to me because it's kind of an entrepreneurial thing. When I got out of school, I planted one church in Canada and another in the United States.

At the same time, I started to realize that a great passion for the field of finance was welling up inside me. At first, I needed to learn finances just to rescue my wife and myself from poverty (which, being a pastor isn't really a solution to poverty, if you didn't know). Then I pursued a master's degree in counseling and things started to come together. I had a ministry mind-set for the kingdom, I had a passion for helping people figure out their finances, and I had a desire to counsel people in their struggles. It all converged for me and I started a company. My wife made it possible because she had a good job in Tennessee, and I was still young and ambitious and thought I could at least give it a whirl, despite knowing that the chances of survival with no seed money to start were not that great.

God gave us favor. We began to build a little company, I asked Jon Maxson to be a partner and we grew, one person at a time. We were basically running it out of the trunks of our cars with no office, no people, no staff, no money, and, my wife might have said at the time, no brains. But I had a lot of drive. From there Beacon Capital Management grew and grew, incredibly multiplied and blessed.

In my work I have been inspired by the book of Acts and what the disciples who followed Jesus did. They were trailblazers and I wanted to be like that. Many of them were tentmakers, or bivocational—meaning that they worked to support themselves and others and then used that income to launch kingdom initiatives.

It doesn't matter whether it's fishing, making tents, or helping people with their finances, discipline and hard work pay off over time and give you the chance to be successful.

From day one, I knew that if I was going to start a company, it was going to be a Christian-based company. I need to clarify what I mean because some people hear "a *Christian* company" and think that means that I am going to be rubbing the gospel in their face. I've learned that you turn people off when that happens. We needed to be competent and intentional and then integrate our faith into our work in a way that makes the service we provide better for people, even if they aren't Christians.

It is not a requirement to have a personal relationship with Jesus to work in our company, but we do let prospective employees know that this is the driving force of the leadership. If they are uncomfortable in a setting where faith is talked about a lot, they may not like it.

We have some office patterns that keep faith in front of us. At 8:30 a.m. on Fridays, all thirty-two of us gather for a stand-up prayer meeting. Everyone is supported and stays connected this way. We can hear their stories and struggles, and their needs are met.

Over time, we were successful enough that we were offered radio time and the opportunity to do a TV show in

Nashville about finances. This was a good chance to integrate our faith into something fairly high profile, but not push people away. So we approached it just like we do everything else: serve the client while allowing our faith to play a role in subtle and intentional ways. We have a "Master's money moment" where we share some Scripture near the end. While that is not the first thing we do, it's enough to work it in there after we have competently helped people. It's one of the most impactful parts of that show and we get amazing feedback on it.

MINISTRY TAKES ON MANY FORMS

One of the unique parts of my journey is that I took a path from being a local church pastor and church planter into the business world. Most people who think about the marketplace have the opposite path. They work in the marketplace and over time start to think of it as ministry and of themselves as a kind of minister, which is great. But for me, I already thought of myself as a minister and then I moved into the marketplace. It wasn't always easy. Ministers often think that such a calling is a lifelong, full-time, vocational calling where your paycheck comes from the church, and I had a lot of really close pastoral friends that were scratching their heads wondering what was really going on with my calling.

A few hung with me, but some people just kind of dropped off the face of the earth. That's unfortunate, although with some years and maturity, I understand the perspective. However, at the time it was tough personally. I questioned myself, wondering if I did something wrong. Was I disappointing God as well as other people?

It is not a requirement to have a personal relationship with Jesus to work in our company, but we do let prospective employees know that this is the driving force of the leadership.

Dr. H. C. Wilson, a leader in The Wesleyan Church, stood by me and supported the move. He said, "Pete, I just want you to know that ministry takes on many different forms. I'm behind you, and I'm proud of you. You didn't leave the ministry; you've just taken a different path of influence in ministry."

FOCUS ON YOUR CIRCLE OF INFLUENCE

I've come to realize that every person has a circle of influence. Whether you work with ten or a thousand people in your company, there's usually four with whom you resonate with, whom you have grown close to. You can't be close to everyone, so you focus on that small group first. If you can't integrate your faith and work with them and influence them for God, then there's no sense in thinking more broadly about your whole company and marketplace. Start small. Start with relationships.

By just being transparent and intentional in praying for and caring for people, coworkers will begin to see that you do things differently, and you do life and work better. This means you can do little things that are naturally part of your conversation to bring up your faith. Don't try to think ahead, manipulate things, or concentrate on certain content to share. Instead, simply share what's already inside of you. If you are a person of faith, it's going to leak out and it's going to show.

I call this approach "pennies in the jar." Just like a kid would save up for something by putting pennies in a jar, I "save up" for future spiritual conversations I'll have with someone by just consistently contributing to their life in a positive and encouraging way. Sometimes it's with a spiritual nuance or a scriptural reference, but oftentimes it's just encouragement. Over time the jar is filled up and it makes a difference. Anyone can do this in any profession. Of course, the core of it is to have credibility in doing your work with excellence. It doesn't work to try to do "Christian work" in the marketplace and then do shoddy professional work. That actually hurts the name of Christ, as if it's a pass for low-quality work. Instead you add value to lives through excellence, then you provide the real eternal value added through the spiritual conversations.

Over time, because of my work, the television show, and publishing some books, I've been able to do some training for financial advisors in larger conferences. It's been helpful in those settings to have a similar approach as the client and coworker conversations and the television show. We establish credibility by helping our peers do financial services better, and then we show how it's integrated with teachings we learn from Scripture. This fascinates people and opens a whole lot of new doors at these conferences. The reality is most of these people in the financial world would not listen to a pastor or someone in another field of work for very long, but by hearing it connected to their own work, it starts to be practical and attractive to them. I love it!

A prayer breakfast is now held at that event and one recently had over 130 people participating. That shows there is a real hunger for how the teachings of God impact the financial services area and that people are willing to go out of their way to hear more.

INFLUENCING YOUR WORK ... INTEGRATING YOUR FAITH

- How can you launch a kingdom initiative in your workplace?
- Ask a trusted advisor at work how you can become a better employee so that you are working at your best to further the kingdom with excellence.

PETE BENSON is a well-known financial expert and the founder and co-owner of Beacon Capital Management, LLC. He is a frequent conference speaker, an author of five financial books, as well as a radio and TV host of his weekly financial show called Beacon Retirement Strategies. Pete serves on several boards, two of which are Kingswood University in Eastern Canada and Southern Wesleyan University in South Carolina. Pete and Ginnie have been married for forty-three years, have three children and seven grandchildren, and live in Franklin (Nashville), Tennessee. They are members of Church of the City. In his spare time, Pete is an avid runner and he and Ginnie love to travel and see new places, especially places with nice weather and a beach.

13
FAITH IS NOT JUST FOR SUNDAYS

*As each has received a gift, use it to serve one another,
as good stewards of God's varied grace.*
—1 Peter 4:10 (ESV)

When I graduated high school in 1999, I figured the future was in computers, so I studied computer information technology in college. I got a great internship at Microsoft and when they offered me a job, I put college on hold and stayed there for four years. In some ways it was the ultimate dream job, but I was in a very technical role there and really wanted to be in project management with more people interaction. So I went back to school to finish my degree and then joined Insurance Management Group (IMG) where I am today.

I started out in sales at the bottom of the barrel and worked my way up on earning credibility because, as I learned, leadership is earned. Later on, I got into operations, and ended up buying the agency in 2015 and took over as president and CEO.

FROM CHASING SUCCESS TO SEEKING CHRIST

I was raised in a great Catholic family, but the focus I picked up on was that my life should revolve around getting a good job. First, get good grades in school, then make money because money means security and that's what you want. My whole life revolved around that goal and it had all worked out because at thirty-four I owned my own successful company. I wasn't buying jets or anything, but I had money, success, and the role I wanted. I had achieved every goal the world might expect of me and would have all the joy and happiness I could ever want. But truthfully, I was more miserable then than I was before.

As I look back, I know I hadn't really given my life to Christ at that point. I was searching for more money and success, but all I felt was more responsibility and less hope. Within

three months of that realization, I met two Christian basketball coaches named Jeff Clark and Greg Tonagel. They
introduced me to a group of people that changed my life. I
discovered through them that serving other people brought
way more joy than serving myself and they helped me learn
how I could pursue Christ and integrate my faith into my
company and with my employees.

I have learned that culture eats strategy for breakfast, and our culture now is what is helping us succeed.

I grew very fast under their discipleship and it began to
change the way I led at work. Work became less stressful
because I surrendered the business to God. Then I started to
wonder if I could create a workplace at IMG where we really
cared about people's growth in a way that changed *their* lives.

REDEFINING GREATNESS

It started with an email to my team. I got everyone in the
room. I already had the love and respect of the people I had
asked to see, so I had a good foundation. I was pretty nervous
and feeling timid because I knew that what I wanted to see
happen was unusual for a company to try. We ultimately

decided to start a Monday morning meeting at our company, which we called "redefining greatness," where we talk about what really matters most in life. At these gatherings, I am able to talk about how my faith drives me and makes our company better.

Early on in these meetings, I explained to the team that Christianity is often viewed like a box. There are things you do, and things you don't do. The things you do are in the box, and the things you don't are out of the box. So if I go to church, if I read the Bible, if I do these things well, then I'm a Christian; I'm in the box. And if I do certain bad things, it means I'm not a Christian and I'm out of the box. Unfortunately, a lot of us in the business world think we live most of life outside of that box. I know my team felt that way.

I stressed to them that the box is a myth. Instead, I like to view Christianity as a line. We're all on a line at different points and we just need to move to the next place of knowing Jesus. For example, if you haven't read the Bible and you don't know the stories well at all, that's OK. Let's just do the next part of the journey. That's the line of your life.

It was also crucial for me to be transparent and real with everyone as I facilitated these meetings. This can be hard for a business leader to do because we want to put up a facade that we've got it all together. But everyone sees through that anyway. I had to be intentional about sharing my struggles and growth. I told them that I was surrendering the company to God and taking a risk with the future.

As we had these meetings, they became more and more of the lifeblood of our company. People's lives were really impacted by it. It was key to not force the conversation, but to allow it to be natural. Of course, I want everyone to change and be saved, but that's not realistic. For me, I was at a different place just two years ago than I am now, and for business leaders and owners who want to integrate their faith and work, these conversations might feel like a massive step, but give it six months and you'll want to keep going.

I can tell you, the fulfillment you'll get from doing something like this is like no other. Think about the lives that could be changed; about the person in your office whose entire life would be transformed if they knew Christ.

Of course, there will always be tension points in any leadership decision. I sense there are still skeptics in the office, and I've learned to be OK with that. I am leading from who I am, and my job is not to place anyone inside or outside of the box. As a leader, I want to continue to meet my people where they are, no matter if they come to the meetings or not. Over time, I trust that credibility will continue to grow as my heart for their growth shows.

One thing that others might worry about is a fear of lack of content. However, the content is not the key; it's your own transparency and openness. That will draw people in. Dig deep in your own soul first. I was fearful at first because I didn't know much about the Bible, and my faith was fairly new. I can't recite verses well enough to answer questions and I worried about being judged, because these people know me, and I'm far from perfect. I wondered, "Are they gonna think it's genuine?"

Over time, I realized that if I just showed up and asked a couple of questions and shared what was going on in my life and heart and let other people do the same, it was amazing on its own. My team loved it. If you walked into our office, you would feel like it's a big family. They know how much they are genuinely cared for. We all want to do a good job and work hard, and we're doing it as a family.

BOTTOM LINE

People wonder, however, what this has meant for business. With this focus on our faith and work, it can make you speculate about the bottom line. Well, our bottom line grew 21 percent last year, so God's expectations have outpaced mine. In reality, I don't focus on that too much because I've given up control and that's not easy to do, especially when you're used to being in control. But when you do, the freedom that comes with that is pretty special.

I have learned that culture eats strategy for breakfast, and our culture now is what is helping us succeed. Our values are "we *wow*, we *team*, we *grow*, and we *serve*." Our mission is to protect and inspire our clients, communities, and coworkers, one interaction at a time. With this in mind, it changes the 100,000 interactions we have a year with clients. It's amazing to have employees who love their jobs, care about the team they are on, are excited about their own growth, and live to serve others.

Sure, any business owner will tell you they want to be profitable in order to be sustainable, but I've learned that there's really no security in most businesses anyway. Anything can happen. Any industry can change. But we all want to run a business that is best in its class. At IMG, we strive for that too. We have dashboards and scoreboards of what success looks like and what goals everybody needs to hit. We compare our numbers against the industry as we aim for excellence, but we don't forget why we're doing it.

From a business systems perspective, I look at it two ways: the science of achievement and the art of fulfillment. The science of achievement is about being successful in this world, and I don't believe that is actually the difficult part.

The biggest failure is when you achieve but are not fulfilled, and I've been there. So at IMG we now know how to achieve and we're going to continue to achieve by God's grace. We believe he's going to bless that and hopefully it goes where we would like it to go. But we have to be willing to accept it if that doesn't happen. We haven't been faced with that yet, but we've surrendered it to him and I'm grateful for all we've been given so far.

INFLUENCING YOUR WORK . . . INTEGRATING YOUR FAITH

- In what ways do you feel fulfilled or unfulfilled in your work?
- What does achievement look like to you?

TRENT DAILEY is a Marion, Indiana, native that attended Marion High School and graduated from Purdue University. He has been married to his wife, Angel, for thirteen years and they have four kids: Roman, Hadley, Eden, and Isaiah. Trent loves spending time with friends and family, going to different events, and traveling the world. His favorite pastime is running with his brothers and friends.

14
PRAYER OPENS DOORS

WAFAA HANNA

Heal the sick [in the house] and say to them,
"The kingdom of God has come near you."
—Luke 10:9 (ESV)

I was born in Egypt and lived there until I was thirty years old. I studied medicine and wanted to become a doctor, so I worked very hard, did my residency, passed all my boards, and did just that.

I found it really difficult to be a Christian in Egypt because it's a mostly Islamic country. You are not supposed to share your faith openly, but I did find that you can live your life in a way that attracts people to ask questions about you and you can answer their questions. Still, even if you are asked about your faith directly, you have to be careful in how you respond. It has to be a testimony, not something where you are very bold in inviting others in. However, I found that if I just loved people, it would make a difference and they would ask enough questions so that I could share my faith.

Many in my extended family had moved to the United States and they, and my husband, Raafat, wanted me to move there too. I didn't really want to leave my country, but I felt that doors kept closing in Egypt and with my own people, and some situations felt like if I chose to be ethical, I would not succeed there, so I became convinced. When I finally did make the move, I had to start all over. I had to do the final exams all over again. I had to do another residency, starting from the bottom and working my way up, and then I took my boards over again. It was a huge challenge to do all that twice.

As I was doing my medical residency, the hospital I was working at offered me a job to stay with them when I completed it. They even gave me a bonus to stay and I have worked at that hospital ever since.

I have felt quite free to express my faith in this role and in this country. I have, I think, a very unique relationship with my patients, because I know a lot about their personal lives and their families. That makes us close and opens the door for a different level of communication. If I am open and honest and taking care of my own spiritual life, it reflects in my work and relationships.

LOVE OPENS DOORS

It's been interesting. Even though I share my faith in my workplace, my colleagues have noticed that patients refer their friends and family to my practice—even people who might not want to hear about my faith, including people from other religions. Then, those new patients refer their family and friends to me as well.

The other doctors in my practice think it is fascinating, and they like, of course, to receive new patients. I think it shows that those you might think would be most offended or most put off by hearing about my faith are in fact those who respond well to my honesty.

One of the things that has healed my soul from the animosity I carried with me from Egypt is my interactions with Muslims in this country. In my home country, I was a part of the oppressed minority, so it was very hard for me to understand the Muslim majority that was so restrictive and demeaning of me. But here, God has opened my eyes to love each Muslim person as an individual. I now treat them with love and tender care. Compassion has replaced my former animosity. When you see a human as a single person, you can become friends and go deeper with them rather than seeing them as a part of some larger group.

TREATING MORE THAN ILLNESS

One of my patients was eighty-two and diagnosed with a very dangerous cancer, which is almost always terminal. She was with me, her two daughters, and several other medical personnel when she was told. Before we even brought it up, she said, "You're gonna tell me I'm gonna die."

At that moment I felt I needed to speak more boldly. I said, "I have something to say to you. It's not up to me or to you as to whether or not you are going to die. I didn't give you your life to tell you that it is going to be taken from you. God can take me before he takes you. Nobody knows. So don't be afraid of me or these other doctors." Then I asked her a question: "What else are you afraid of?"

She said, as you might expect, "I don't want to die." I asked her why she was afraid of death. She told me it was because she didn't know where she was going, and she didn't know about the afterlife. This is, of course, not territory the doctors in the room were used to being in. We usually stay out of such discussions. But there she was, sitting on the exam table in front of me with her daughters close by. I pulled my chair right close, looking up at her on the exam table. I got very close to her and I put my hand on her shoulder. I said, "Let me tell you something. I know where I'm going, I am going to heaven."

She replied, "How do you know?"

I told her I had decided to follow Jesus, and then I gave a very simple story in just two minutes, the whole good news of Jesus in a nutshell. She told me she didn't like churches and Christians, and I said, "This isn't about the church or Christians. I'm a lover of Jesus. I love him because of what he did for me."

She asked me, "How can I make this decision?" With her daughters and the doctors around us, we had a holy moment

When you see a human as a single person, you can become friends and go deeper with them rather than seeing them as a part of some larger group.

/ / / / / / / / / / / / / / / / /

together where she prayed after me and talked to God. Whether she died the next day or in ten years, she knew she was right with God.

I have found that praying for people can be the best way for me to relate to them about spiritual things. Those who don't believe in God or who believe in other religions don't mind it if you ask if you can pray for them. It is a nonaggressive and positive way to share faith.

I had another patient that was a very, very successful millionaire. I couldn't quite figure out why he was coming to me for help. He didn't have a real medical problem. He said, "I don't know what's wrong with me, but I'm not myself." When I asked him to tell me more, he said, "I have the biggest house in the area, I am wealthy beyond belief, and I'm successful at what I do. But I don't have the relationships I want, with family or anyone else. I can't figure out what's missing." I asked him about depression and other things, and we talked for a long time.

Eventually in our conversations I told him, "I think there is a vacuum in your heart. You're missing something big." I asked if he had a Bible at home and when he replied that he did not, I got him one from my office. I asked him to start in

/ /

the book of John and I showed him where it was in the Bible; I told him to call me if he had any questions about it. I did put him on an antidepressant as that was needed, but that wasn't the only thing. His prescription was more than pills, it was the good news.

GOD'S REDEMPTION PLAN IN ACTION

One of the great joys of my life now is that my husband and I were part of starting a new church in Midtown Detroit called Mosaic Church. Our dream is to include people of every nation, every socioeconomic group, and every educational background. And it's happening. We have people that are very rich in the church sitting next to somebody who is basically homeless, and you really don't feel a big difference because we are a family. Everybody is very sensitive to where others are coming from. America might not be a melting pot, but our church is.

I have found that being a physician can be a double-edged sword. It can draw people toward you or push them away. How you present yourself to people sets it up. I just need to be like Jesus and love people and love my community. I have found that I can use my background to reach out to people and love them not only in my work, but also in my church. We have a real desire to be hospitable, since we have people in our church from many countries. Many times, immigrant families feel rejected or unwanted and we can share in their heartache that way. My accent can actually help me with some of these people, whereas it hurts me in other situations. They notice my accent and they know immediately that I'm like them. I sometimes play a little game with people and make them try to guess my accent and what country I'm from. Most people don't guess Egypt. It's fun and breaks the ice.

I wish more people would know what a difference a new church like this can make. We knew that this city needed a new multiethnic church, one that reached out to people that were at a major financial disadvantage. Many generations of hardship are found here, and we want to be a part of seeing that turn around.

In order for that to happen we need to be here to learn from each other and serve each other, because many people here were never allowed to be themselves—they weren't safe to be themselves, We want to help people feel empowered to reverse poverty, to overcome the abuse they suffered or whatever challenges they face. We know Jesus can help.

Not long ago, we became connected to a heroin addict. His wife was clean, and she was trying to help him. He has two boys, so we invited them all over for dinner. It was great to cook for them and it gave us space to have a great conversation. He told us that he had never been in an American house in his life. No one had ever cooked for him. All he ever knew was canned food.

A home-cooked meal and a welcoming attitude can be part of the solution, but it is the love of Jesus that moves my heart in the first place and causes action. Perhaps for you it will be different ideas and actions of compassion, but they must all start in the same place: experiencing the love of Jesus and wanting to share it. It has been very rewarding to experience this myself and be able to connect with people in their real lives and see God redeem wrongs and make people whole.

- How can you speak boldly in the workplace while being respectful to the environment?
- Who do you have animosity toward that you could begin to treat with compassion?

/ / / / / / / / / / / / / / /

DR. WAFAA HANNA *was born to a Christian family and raised in Egypt. Her father died from a brain hemorrhage while teaching in a classroom. Only after this event did she feel the need to be close to her heavenly Father, and she received him as her personal Savior. She has been led by God through an amazing life journey, spiritually, academically, and socially, and now serves as a doctor in Detroit, Michigan, where she lives with her husband, Raafat. They are founding members of Mosaic Church in Midtown Detroit.*

15
ADORE THE BLESSER

OMAR HAEDO

Give, and it will be given to you. A good measure, pressed down, shaken together and running over, will be poured into your lap. For with the measure you use, it will be measured to you.
—Luke 6:38

In 1987, I was just a punk kid without much possibility ahead of me. I heard that a big company was doing job interviews at a school I wasn't even attending. I was motivated and decided to go for it. I had to make some chavos somehow or I couldn't pay the bills. It was either this or sell fried chicken.

When I got to the school, I couldn't get in the main entrance because I didn't have the right ID. I went around the side where there was a huge fence. I climbed over the fence, then walked across the campus like I belonged there.

I found the interview location and introduced myself. They thought I was a nice guy, but when they realized I wasn't a student there, they asked, "How did you get in here?"

"Well, I sort of jumped the fence because I really wanted this job."

Apparently, they liked my answer because they didn't kick me out. The man who was interviewing me then asked, "How do you feel about discrimination in the workplace?"

I thought about that question and reflected on my background. I told him, "Well, I grew up on an island of diversity—literally, because Puerto Rico is an island. I suppose that before you asked me that question, I hadn't thought much about you being black. I was so nervous because I need this job, so I'm not really thinking about that right now."

I wasn't sure if this was a good answer or not, it's just what I blurted out at the time. He started to tear up and smiled at me, and I got the job. That's how my fence-jumping career got a jump start.

A WORK IN PROGRESS

After working hard at that company for several years and doing a lot of good work for them, I decided it was time to set up my own business.

In many ways, it felt like starting over. I stirred up the pot in the insurance business in Puerto Rico, and everyone seemed to be against me. I was terrified and didn't think I was going to make it. I went into my closet on my knees and prayed to God, "I'm a child of the King. This is your company, not mine. You motivated me to take this risk. I don't know if it's your will. I can't see the horizon over the waves, but I am asking for angels to surround me."

What happened next is an experience I will always remember. I literally felt wings brush up against my body as I prayed. I felt God's presence cover me like never before. Ever since then, I've known that I can call upon the name of the Lord, because my identity is a child of God.

God blessed us and our business for twenty years. It was amazing. It shook up the insurance world on the islands in the Caribbean for a long time. Some people still use the phrases BO and AO—before Omar and after Omar.

But of course, that's what got me into trouble. Thinking it was all about me. Eventually I started to adore the blessings more than the Blesser.

We human beings are really good at creating idols. My priorities were out of whack. I had the corner office, the penthouse, and more grown-up toys than I could count. God began to convict me of all this, and I realized God wanted me to be an entrepreneur and take risks for him again. So I sold off the company and the success. I went from feeling like somebody to feeling like nobody again. Once again, I started over.

But that was good. It was good to no longer be a big shot. It was good to get back to that kid who would jump fences to get in. I've learned that Jesus still walks on the water and he is going to walk over the biggest problem you have in front of you. I started reminding myself that I might sink but I'd still be OK because Jesus is out on that water before me.

In starting a new insurance company, I wanted to be sure I didn't do the idol thing again. At one point, we bid on a huge account, but did not secure it. I was angry and disappointed, but I said, "OK, God, this is your company, maybe this isn't your will." I saw this as a test. I had to trust God because he sees the full picture, not me.

One month later, Hurricane Maria hit the Caribbean. If we had carried that huge account, our company would have been easily destroyed. God was protecting us; I'm sure of it. Through that I learned that God is fine with my doubt and anger. He knows more than I do; I just have to give it over to him. I learned to live by Psalm 84:11: "The Lord God is a sun and shield . . . no good thing does he withhold from those whose walk is blameless." I read this as God being my sun of direction and my shield of protection.

After the hurricane, we sprang into action—not just for business, but to help people. We found a wealthy guy with a jet who helped us take diabetes supplies out to the islands. During those emergency days, we weren't counting the cost on our own balance sheets—we were just trying to help others in need. Then the guy with the jet told me, "Some of my relief workers need a place to stay while they are responding. Can you move your boat to near where they live so they can stay there?" I owed this fella since he was helping us move 500,000 dollars' worth of supplies to the islands, so I took the time to take it down there, thinking it was just a gift since we were all working toward helping others.

He called me back later and asked, "How does $60,000 a month sound to rent your boat for the relief workers?"

He rented it for three months and because of that I was able to make payroll salaries for my entire staff in a completely unexpected way during the worst time in our business.

A MATTER OF CHARACTER

That experience taught me a lot about being a God-trusting entrepreneur. If doing something is scary, hard, requires grit, creativity, growth, and discipline, that's where I can chase God's will. It's tempting to find something safe and easy rather than scary and hard, but if God tells us his road is narrow, why do we always think he'll bless us when we walk the wide road?

I've learned that Jesus still walks on the water and he is going to walk over the biggest problem you have in front of you.

The business world is a swamp full of snakes on one side of the boat and alligators on the other. People can be brutal and treasonous. But if you stick to the straight and narrow, the reputation and character of your work starts to become a selling point.

Recently, I was advising a CEO on his choices. I gave him option A and option B, and option B was me and my company.

I was honest and straightforward about the options. I didn't throw the other company under the bus, I just told him what was good about each. After doing that, I didn't think we would get the account. The competition was a good option for him, and he would have to leave the other company for us.

The CEO came back and shocked me by saying he was going with us. He told me, "You've educated us on the options, you're transparent about ups and downs in this industry. We're choosing you because of the way you operate." That's how I've learned that the power of persuasion is limited compared to the power of transparent truth. We just have to be really good at what we do, and then be truthful and wise.

The motto of my work is, "Winning by doing what's right." To be honest, I'm not always sure what the right thing is, but I know what it is *not* when I see it, so the right things come by process of elimination. This means that at town hall meetings where important business decisions are made in terms of policy, I act boldly. It means we educate, help, and mentor whoever needs it in order to help the customer or client win.

It also means treating people with honor and respect. More often than not, my faith comes up in the workplace because of ethics. I always say there are no ethics tests in the workplace—there are only character pop quizzes, and you pass or fail based on who you have allowed yourself to become.

When one of my employees calls and says, "So-and-so scored a big sale from a competitor who badmouths us," I use that as a coaching moment. Yes, we should celebrate, but not because we're happy that the competition lost. We don't want to lose God's favor because our hearts are in the wrong place. The same is true when we lose; we can't despair then either.

I've been in phone meetings where someone starts bad-mouthing someone else who isn't on the call and I speak up and say, "I understand that you have feelings about that person, but my life is too rich to talk about someone else this way so I'm gonna hang up now." This can get you a lot of enemies who may think, "Who does this guy think he is?" But it also buys you admiration and loyalty. Even that person you shut down knows you're not talking about *them* behind their backs either, and they might not know that about even one other person in this whole world.

When I was growing up, a pastor told me that I should be a pastor. He was chagrined when I didn't want to be and I told him about my business inclinations. Over time, I've begun to see how the lines blur about who is a minister and who isn't. I like to view all I do as a way of contributing to the kingdom, and not just because money is made and I give some away to "ministries." It's because my actual business work contributes to making the world a better place and even saves lives from time to time. While that might not be "ministry" in the way some seminaries define it, it's still discipling and multiplying the kingdom. Maybe ministry doesn't need a steeple on top to be holy.

I have a friend who is the worldwide benefits director for a Fortune 50 company. He recently told me, "I am leading like you advised me: Just do the right thing and put it in God's hands. I do that daily and I will tell you, I am happier now than I've been in twenty years."

GENEROSITY SPEAKS VOLUMES

Working in the business world can feel like climbing a wall of manure at times, but I have found that no matter what people may believe, they are intrigued and drawn in by your generosity. Most leaders are so self-centered that they can't believe someone is happy and not self-centered, and chooses to give away money, time, and control.

Right after Hurricane Maria, I drove a truck all over the Bahamas for two days with World Hope International because they had generators, air filters, and water bladders in staging areas and could not distribute materials fast enough for relief. My non-Christian clients and colleagues were baffled that anyone would do something like that and be happy doing it. Generosity cuts through a lot of talk and proves your character in the marketplace. You can tell a person's heart by where their time and money go, and that's true for those who don't believe in God, too. They might not believe your words, but they can see your actions.

For me, the inner resources to sustain this way of life in the marketplace comes from having a life of prayer. We can move the hand of God in prayer. It's like WD-40 on joints—it gets things moving. Prayer early in the day gives you words later in the day for those character pop quizzes.

I look at it this way: I'm an airplane pilot, which is quite convenient for my island-hopping work, but also a ton of fun for me. I've learned that when the engine quits up in the air, you don't have time to read the instructions; you act immediately to fix the problem. In the same way I ask myself, "What am I drawing from? What is the margin in my life that is spiritual?" Without that, my life will drop out of the sky like a plane with a broken-down engine.

- How can you become more generous with your time, money, and control?
- Is there something in your workplace that does not honor others? How can you address it?

OMAR HAEDO, *GBA, is the president and CEO of Elan Insurance Group. He serves on the boards of World Hope International, Houghton College, and Immigrant Connection. He was a former partner in Medical Air Services Association and managing principal at IKON Group. Omar is married to Liza and is the proud father of five children. You can follow Omar on Twitter at @OHaedo.*

16
INFLUENCE THROUGH HEALING

SCOTT ADDISON

> *If you are faithful in little things, you will be faithful in large ones. But if you are dishonest in little things, you won't be honest with greater responsibilities.*
> —Luke 16:10 (NLT)

I've been a family physician for twenty years in Muskegon, Michigan, caring for patients from newborns to people in their nineties, including some four-generation families. In addition to this work, I have two big volunteer roles: I work with Young Life locally, and I provide leadership to Global Partners Health Network, a network of Wesleyans who want to impact health and bring healing to communities around the world while introducing the good news to them.

I feel like God has put me in my local practice in Michigan to take care of people. Not just provide health care, but really love them. From time to time I sense being led to share my faith with my patients, asking, "Is this OK for me to share?"

I almost always get a yes to that, and then I will give them some encouragement or let them know I am praying for them and they may even invite me to pray with them right then and there. Whenever someone knows they are prayed for, I find that they are appreciative of the consideration, even if they don't believe in God.

As I do this work, I've often wondered about Luke, who wrote two books of the Bible, traveled with Paul, and was also a physician. I always wondered if Paul recruited Luke to go because he was a doctor. Perhaps he said to Luke, "Well, my friend, if my track record is any indicator, I think I might get beat up a lot on this trip, so I hope you come with me because I'm gonna need a doctor."

My local practice is part of my work for God, but I try to give my energy to the health missions work as well. I take Tuesdays and Thursday afternoons off from the doctor's office and commit those days to these volunteer efforts. There are other times when it creeps into my life, but those times are specifically designated for it. It might involve thinking through our need for a pharmacist at Zimba Mission Hospital in Zambia, or trying to schedule doctor and nurse trips to another field for the next year, or working with a church in the US to find ways to impact the health of a refugee camp in Mozambique.

It has been so helpful through the years to have Dennis Jackson, who used to be my local church pastor and is now the head of Global Partners, to encourage this way of life. He poured time into me, taking me on mission trips and empowering me to lead in the world in a way that uses my vocation as a doctor.

Global Partners Health Network (GPHN) grew from recognizing the needs out there to finding ways to fill some of

My work in America supports the work in other countries, and the work in other countries reinforces and repositions my focus in America.

/ / / / / / / / / / / / / / /

those needs. We want to unleash people to meet some very key needs around the world and we want people to learn about Jesus Christ, but oftentimes we need to fulfill some basic physical needs so that they are even alive to hear of Jesus in the first place.

HEAL FIRST, LIKE JESUS DID

It can feel overwhelming when we think of all the needs, of course. A GPHN member who is an ophthalmologist from California has made countless trips to Africa; he even built an eye hospital in Zambia. Because of his commitment and sacrifices, patients who are completely blind due to cataracts can now have their sight restored with a procedure that takes minutes to perform. Others die from easily treatable diseases. Daily, babies are dying all over the world from diarrhea, many who would live if they had access to IV fluids. The needs are profound, and the solutions are relatively simple. Everyone has some skill, gift, or resource that can be used to meet health needs around the world. We are trying our best, and see lives transformed and literally saved in this life, and sometimes in the next life, through the holistic introduction of faith to people in these communities.

We often gloss over the fact that when Jesus came to Israel, he would heal people first and then share the good news with them. The first time Jesus sent out his disciples he told them to heal people first. As medical professionals, we take that instruction literally. It is something really profound to heal, and we don't want to take that for granted.

People who choose a career in health care want to help people and we want to empower them to help people worldwide, in places where people are in dire need. We have found that people grow significantly through this work, no matter where they are in their faith journey.

LOVING AND OBEYING

When I come back to my own practice in Michigan, it reminds me that people are people everywhere. I shouldn't be more faithful or obedient when I'm doing medical missions in some other country. I should have the same motivation whether I'm in Mozambique or Muskegon. The person I meet in my office is someone I should love and treat with dignity and I should want them to hear about Jesus just like someone overseas. That patient is a child of God, just the same.

My work in America supports the work in other countries, and the work in other countries reinforces and repositions my focus in America. The way I integrate my faith here should be the same as it is over there and that's more than just what I do in my work as a family physician. It should be integrated in my relationship with my wife, kids, church, and neighborhood. I should be the same guy in all situations. God is in it all and he is paying attention to it all. That is what integrity is all about.

Jesus made it clear that we are to love God and love our neighbors. I find that starts with loving whomever God has put in front of me. That might be someone on a phone call, a family member, a patient here in Michigan, or a medical missionary serving overseas, but it might also be a person who is upset at the bank or the child of a friend I meet in the neighborhood. Love who is in front of you . . . right then!

Listening and obeying in the little things leads to a lot of other possibilities in your life. If you listen to God's little asks, then as the big asks come in you're more sensitive to the Spirit in the moment.

The tendency is to wait for the big asks and ignore the little ones. Instead, Jesus taught us, "If you are faithful in little things, you will be faithful in large ones. But if you are dishonest in little things, you won't be honest with greater responsibilities" (Luke 16:10 NLT).

INFLUENCING YOUR WORK . . . INTEGRATING YOUR FAITH

- What do you give your time and effort to outside of the workplace?
- Are you integrating the same amount of faithfulness and passion in all areas of your life?

DR. SCOTT ADDISON *is a family physician, husband of more than twenty-six years to Sheila, father of three sons, director of Global Partners Health Network, and wannabe chef.*

17
LEAD DIFFERENTLY

ESTHERLITA GRIFFITHS

Therefore go and make disciples of all nations . . . teaching
them to obey everything I have commanded you.
And surely I am with you always, to the very end of the age.
—Matthew 28:18–20

Soon after I became a divisional vice president at Sears Canada, I was asked to take on a new project to outsource almost all of the company's information technology operations function to a major consulting firm. In addition to the functions that I was hired to lead (architecture, project management, governance), the CIO asked that I take responsibility for compiling and reporting IT finances and facilitating the transition to the consulting firm.

Imagine being in the room when a hundred people found out they were going to lose their jobs in the next three months. How do you "lead differently" as a Christian when so many are losing their jobs? As you can imagine, many were extremely angry. Others were bewildered at the prospect of finding a new job after twenty, thirty, forty years in a role and no experience with LinkedIn and the other contemporary approaches to marketing one's skills. I had "lived experience" as an employee when the financial services organization I had worked for earlier in my career was acquired by a larger company. I began to pray and ask God to give me wisdom to face the journey.

TO LEAD DIFFERENTLY

I found that one real way I could work with integrity as a Christian was to be as transparent as possible about the process while observing my responsibilities as a leader within the organization. Yes, I wanted to help people cope with the decision and show sympathy and empathy, but it was important that I speak the truth while I kept the company's information and the employees' responses confidential. The barriers and posturing on both sides of me seemed high and insurmountable. (Each employee's release date was confidential with the company, and my communication with them was limited to what was predetermined by HR.)

I quickly built relationships with the five managers and explained that we needed to have weekly meetings every Friday where I could be visible to everyone, answer questions, and address concerns. I was also looking for opportunities to retain some of the employees for the next era into which we were entering. In doing so, I was constantly juggling the need to be empathetic and transparent, while also evaluating talent for the future.

I was intentional about connecting with love and confidence with both the managers and their staff, and found ways in which I could be their advocate while also being a part of the leadership transition team. I shared from my personal experiences and encouraged them to see me and HR if they needed help in preparing for next steps.

One of the managers subsequently shared her appreciation for the ways in which I was leading the team through that challenging time. She and others understood the tension I was living with and could read between the lines. She told me, "No one in leadership in these situations, and certainly not in this one, has been willing to face us and be open with us."

I assured her that I was drawing on my past experiences to assist her and others in preparing for next steps. I explained, "While I can't share all the details, I want to help you prepare for your next steps. I want you to be able to make the best of this." Similarly, I shared with the entire team that, while unpleasant, this situation presented an opportunity for them and their families to experience something different. "You can walk out that door one, two, or three months from now with referrals and resumes and networking. Take advantage

of this season if you can. The company is providing resources to help you and I'm here to help as well," I said.

There is no prescription to solve these kinds of leadership challenges, but it's important to be open to the Holy Spirit's guidance and be aware that God is working before we even notice it. We must remember that every situation we face can be a moment for God to show up in the marketplace. We need to keep our eyes and heart open.

TRANSPARENCY IN LEADERSHIP AND FAITH

Transparency during that situation was important, as well as demonstrating my faith in the marketplace. I know that some leaders feel it is difficult to share personal faith in their vocation, but the way I see it, I am merely sharing what is important to me, what is a part of me, and essentially who I am. It would be strange (and unacceptable to me) if someone who had worked with me for years discovered that faith had been a huge part of my life only when attending my funeral.

People share their personal lives all the time at work. If I never shared about my faith, then others might conclude that it was not that important to me. They might hear that I "go to church," but they might never understand what a relationship with Jesus means to me and how it leads me to act or respond.

I think it starts with demonstrating my love of Christ and being open to sharing why it matters so much to me. I had a coworker who said, "I've seen how you're operating in this negative season of business life and I want to know what it means to have faith."

That's the effect I want to have on people. I want them to see that my faith is making me different, and also learn enough about what I've shared about my personal faith to know that I love Jesus and ask about it. I don't want them to just think that I am a special person or a really good person. No, I want them to give me permission to share more about why Jesus is the reason I'm different.

A Muslim coworker of mine, who I'll call Kali, once told me, "You know, I can tell that you are who you are because of your faith." That is the effect I pray for. I want my demonstration of love for others to be a tangible expression of my faith and my relationship with Christ. The key is to do both—share my faith and love others.

> *. . . when we interact with people, we need to view their whole life, not just one facet of it.*

When Kali's mother passed away, it was important for me to make the time to be with her when she was laying her mom to rest. I did not know what to expect as I prepared to join her and her family in the mosque that morning. However, as I took my shoes off and sat with them, I felt an inexplicable peace and that I was where I needed to be.

In another instance, I hired a young consultant contractor to work with us on a software implementation. Normally, you don't spend time coaching and mentoring a contractor; they are hired with the skills to perform a role, execute, and move on. However, I sensed the need to provide guidance regarding specific political nuances to ensure the success of the initiative.

In talking to him, he spoke highly of his mom's Muslim faith. When possible, I would share my faith, including Scripture, without any offence to him (in fact, he knew scriptures as well). I stayed in touch at the end of his consulting contract and have maintained a great networking relationship over the years. He's an expert in his field and I've been able to refer him to other companies with outstanding results.

Recently, he was reminiscing about the projects we've worked on in the past: "Remember how there was so much stress in that office, and we were talking about God?" He respected me highly as a manager, yet what struck him the most was our discussions about faith. The story is not over for our connection; who knows what God might do because I transparently share my faith with him.

DISCIPLESHIP IN THE MARKETPLACE

Earlier in my career I was associate vice president for solution architecture and information security at Canadian Tire. I managed a team of about twenty people and was implementing a new "architect-in-training" program and hiring new architects to ensure I had the resources to meet the demand. One of the new hires was a young Hispanic man (whom I'll call Juan) with a wealth of experience in the business and great aptitude for becoming a solution architect. After his initial presentation of a proposed solution to the Architecture Review Board, I offered feedback regarding his body language and how that would have impacted perceptions about his self-confidence and the viability of the proposed solution. With greater awareness and additional coaching, including examples of how I combined my faith and technology skills to grow as a leader, I saw how he demonstrated greater self-confidence and grew over time.

About five years later, I was back in Toronto and working with Sears Canada. I visited a church in the community where I lived and thought I saw Juan. I actually lingered in my vehicle at the end of the service and, as I was preparing to leave, saw him again and made a beeline to him. We had a wonderful time catching up and I learned that he had not only grown in his work life with the coaching I had given him, but that this had also expressed itself in his development as a speaker and a leader in his church, where he was now a bivocational pastor.

Each of these examples provides me with a powerful confirmation of how important it is for me to "lead differently" and be open and transparent about my faith, to demonstrate "love in action" to everyone with whom I engage, and to coach and mentor even where I have no "mandate" or idea of what kind of impact I could have on someone's life. I continue to look for opportunities to serve those with whom I engage in the marketplace without focusing solely on "work life." That's the point: when we interact with people, we need to view their whole life, not just one facet of it.

I've always sensed God's pleasure and blessing over what I do. There are times when I've wondered if a particular detour was part of his will, and he has confirmed each time that "he is in it" and "he is enough," especially when a situation seems unmanageable. Consequently, I don't feel like I couldn't or shouldn't be a part of God's plan as he reveals himself and his desire for me to serve in the marketplace or in discipling people.

I have never felt that God's command in Matthew 28 to go and make disciples was not part of his purpose for me as an individual. So I encourage you to go and make disciples as well. Go now. Go where you live and work. Start where you are. You might not know where it will take you, or when and how it will change lives. That does not matter. Trust God to show you each step, each day.

INFLUENCING YOUR WORK . . . INTEGRATING YOUR FAITH

- How have you led with integrity and transparency through a tough transition?
- What aspects of Estherlita's example would you bring into a tough situation at work?

ESTHERLITA GRIFFITHS and her husband, Emile, currently live in Calgary, Alberta (Canada). She is an accomplished leader who has over twenty-five years of experience in information technology, and project and change management across the finance, retail, and nonprofit sectors. She is a coach, advisor, and consultant, and has a passion for helping individuals and organizations advance their core capabilities and elevate their impact.

Appendix 1A
STARTING YOUR OWN LOCAL CHAPTER OF MARKETPLACE MULTIPLIERS

SUMMARY*

A local chapter is a gathering of marketplace Christians who influence their workplace and integrate their faith by making disciples and unleashing the kingdom of God wherever they are. Your chapter will work to connect these people together and equip them to do this to the best of their ability. Your local chapter will help each marketplace multiplier know they aren't in this alone and help them increase their intentionality in their workplace.

A local chapter works to:

- Gather marketplace Christians who influence their workplace and integrate their faith
- Show marketplace multipliers they aren't in this alone
- Help increase intentionality in the workplace

STEP 1—
Register Your Chapter at MarketplaceMultipliers.com.

STEP 2—
Make a List of mentors, church leaders, community leaders, neighbors, family, colleagues, and other leaders to invite.

STEP 3—
Pray over your names.

STEP 4—
Partner with someone who can help you lead.

STEP 5—
Plan how your local chapter meetings will work (location, logistics, refreshments, seating, discussion, content, and name of the local chapter).

STEP 6—
Schedule your meetings.

STEP 7—
Contact the people on your list, explain the purpose of your proposed meeting, and invite them.

STEP 8—

Start with your first meeting and take note of what works well and what you can do better next time.

STEP 9—

Practice by getting better from week to week. Make little adjustments to how things go in order to improve meetings.

STEP 10—

Be Faithful and Fruitful by encouraging those on your list, whether they come to the chapter meetings or not.

The fruit you are seeking from the seeds you plant may not come right away. It may take some time, but when you are faithful, over time, God will give you the fruit he intends for you to harvest. You might plant seeds, others might water them, and still others may harvest them—but know that God is the one who makes everything grow. Trust God for that fruit. Enjoy the faithful and fruitful journey in God!

*See the following appendix, 1B, for a full description of each of these steps.

Appendix 1B
STARTING YOUR OWN LOCAL CHAPTER OF MARKETPLACE MULTIPLIERS

A local chapter is a gathering of marketplace Christians who influence their workplace and integrate their faith by making disciples and unleashing the kingdom of God wherever they are. Your chapter will work to connect these people together and equip them to do this to the best of their ability. Your local chapter will help each marketplace multiplier know they aren't in this alone and help them increase their intentionality in their workplace.

At the end of this appendix, you will understand the steps and factors for launching a local chapter of marketplace multipliers who you know and actually start a meeting with those people.

STEP 1—Register Your Chapter

Go to MarketplaceMultipliers.com and register your intent to start a chapter. This will connect you to useful tools, stories from other chapters, and inspiring ideas you can implement in your context. You don't need to know everything about your chapter to register it. You just need to share some core information about yourself to do so.

STEP 2—Make a List

Who would be the best people to invite into your local chapter? Below is a space to write their names. To get you started, think of friends of yours:

MENTORS: Marketplace leaders who have invested in you in the past

CHURCH LEADERS: Those on your church board or other leaders at your church who also have a role in the marketplace

COMMUNITY LEADERS: Those who are known in your community and already have influence, who are also Christians

NEIGHBORS: Christians you live near or interact with in your immediate community

FAMILY: Those related to you that have these instincts to integrate their faith at work and influence people for Christ (including immediate family members)

COLLEAGUES: Those at your workplace who are Christians and might help you start this

LEADERS: Those who could help you lead (see "Partner" below)

Make a list of those people you might invite here:

STEP 3—Pray

The first thing to do with your list is to pray over your names. Pray that God would move in the hearts of those you are taking the initiative to talk to and invite into starting this local chapter with you.

Thank—Be grateful to God for each of the people on your list. Thank God for the opportunity to participate with his activity in the world.

Ask—Make requests of God for the lives of those on your list. Ask God to give you wisdom as you start a local marketplace multiplier chapter.

Praise—As opportunities arise to connect with those on your list, give God praise. Praise God for the love and truth he has shown you.

Write out a short two- to three-sentence prayer for wisdom in starting your local chapter:

STEP 4—Partner

It may be helpful to find someone to partner with you in starting this local chapter. By not "going it alone" and sharing the facilitation duties, it can lessen the weight on your shoulders. It can also help you be consistent to meet regularly even if you happen to be out of town at a scheduled meeting time. If you have a partner, they can lead without you there.

Write down names of people with whom you might meet with to discuss your dreams for marketplace influence and ask if they might partner with you in leading it:

STEP 5—Plan

Think through how your local chapter meetings will work. Where will you meet? How many people do you expect, minimum and maximum? Will you serve refreshments? Tea and coffee? Will you ask anyone to bring anything? How will you guide the discussion? Do you have a name for your group? (You don't need to call it "Marketplace Multipliers," you could call it whatever you like.)

Elements to potentially include:

Inspiration

- Opening prayer: This could be a role for your pastor to play in blessing the meeting and letting people know she or he is supportive of this work.
- Planned stories: When you hear of someone that has had a breakthrough or key moment at work, invite them to prepare to share it for three to five minutes.
- Hot-seat prayer: When someone shares a particular struggle or request, right then and there have that person sit in a chair in the middle of the room and pray over them as a group.
- Prepared talk: Invite a well-known person to speak to your group for ten to thirty minutes.

Information

- Distribute handouts: Provide something of more detail for people to digest and read when they head home or go to work.
- Read a book together: Walk through a chapter a month or use some other format.
- Watch a video: Find a resource that would go deeper into some subject brought up at a prior meeting.

Interaction

- Introductions and updates: Go around the room to hear where each person works and how they are integrating their faith and work and influencing others for Christ.

- Break into smaller discussion groups: Having more than ten people in a group makes interaction more difficult. Consider pairing up or breaking into groups of three to five people.
- Break into smaller prayer groups: Again, people may be more willing to share prayer requests and pray in front of others if paired up or in a smaller group.

Invitation

- Ask all present to commit to some action by the next meeting. This ensures that the meetings are not just social but action-oriented and committed to results.
- Invite people to start their own small meeting in their workplace to make disciples and multiply the kingdom there.
- Remind them of future meeting plans and ask them to not only be there but to invite others to participate that fit the makeup of your group.

STEP 6—Schedule

Figure out what day or night of a typical week works best for you to schedule your meetings. What's the best time not just for you but for the people you want to include in this? Once this is scheduled, clear that in your calendar for several months. It is also important to find a starting date to launch with your first meeting. Be sure to get your partner or others you are inviting that are closest to you to commit to this date first.

STEP 7—Contact

It's time to reach out to the people on your list. Send texts and emails, preferably one-on-one, not groups, and make the invite. Some you may want to meet with face-to-face and others you could call. The key is to make this a personal invitation, not a general "Y'all come" on social media. Give each person the specific start and end times, address, and a sense of what the gathering will feel like. Be low-key with this invitation—it is not a huge deal and high pressure—it's just an invitation to gather with you for the purpose you indicate.

Part of this contact should "start where they are at." What is it that will connect them to your gathering? It could be many things:

Community—Some are just looking for friendships and connection with others. They may feel lonely in the task of integrating their faith and work.

Curiosity—Some would like to learn more about this subject.

Depth—Some might already have made this a way of life and want to go deeper into it instead of just listening to others talk about it.

Questions—Some might have specific questions that they are hoping to find answers for.

Problems—Some have problems unique to their kind of working environment and they are searching for solutions to those problems.

STEP 8—Start

Hold your first meeting and take note of what works well and what you can do better next time. The good thing is that this small meeting is not a big deal and not everything rides on it. If the starting gathering isn't all that great, it's not the end of the world . . . you've got the next meeting scheduled!

This is another reason not to delay starting too long. It's better to just start and get going rather than wait. There is not a lot of risk to this kind of launch, so better to just dive in and figure it out along the way.

STEP 9—Practice

Practice makes perfect. Well, you're not quite aiming for perfection in your gatherings, but you do want it to get better from week to week. After each meeting, reflect on how your gathering went and what you might like to do differently the next meeting. Nothing teaches like experience. Your context is different than that of others. Make little adjustments to how things go in order to improve from week to week.

STEP 10—Be Faithful and Fruitful

Your biggest job as a local chapter leader is to be a faithful friend and to encourage those on your list, whether they come to the chapter meetings or not.

Over time, keep growing your list of those who could be marketplace multipliers if they were intentional about it. If you are a good friend, eventually some will respond to your invitation to join the chapter.

It will be key to just meet consistently and be a transforming presence in your community as marketplace multipliers. There is something noble and trustworthy about being consistent in the lives of those on your list.

Appendix 2A
STARTING YOUR OWN GATHERING AT WORK

SUMMARY*

Starting a gathering at your workplace can be broken down into a step-by-step process. It has some similarities to launching a local marketplace multipliers chapter, so if you've already done that you've practiced some of the activities that will make this easier.

STEP 1—

Get Advice from Others in your local chapter or at MarketplaceMultipliers.com.

STEP 2—

Define the Purpose of Your Gathering to clarify what you are aiming at and inviting people into. It could be an outreach group, Bible study, book study, microchurch, Q&A group, etc.

STEP 3—

Make a List of the best people to invite into your gathering.

STEP 4—

Pray over your names.

STEP 5—

Partner with someone to help you lead the gatherings.

STEP 6—

Plan how your marketplace gathering will work. Consider location, refreshments, preparation, discussion, content, and format.

STEP 7—

Schedule what day or night of a typical week works best for you and others.

STEP 8—

Contact those on your list with the details.

STEP 9—
   Start by having your first meeting and take note of what works well and what you can do better next time.

STEP 10—
   Practice over time and get better with each meeting.

STEP 11—
   Be Faithful and Fruitful by encouraging those on your list, whether they come to the marketplace gatherings or not.

*See the following appendix, 2B, for a full description of each of these steps.

STARTING YOUR OWN GATHERING AT WORK

"And Jesus came and said to them, 'All authority in heaven and on earth has been given to me. Therefore go and make disciples of all nations, baptizing them in the name of the Father and of the Son and of the Holy Spirit, and teaching them to obey everything I have commanded you. And surely I am with you always, to the very end of the age'" (Matt. 28:18–20).

As you take up the call to "go and make disciples" among the people of your workplace, it might be difficult to know where to start. This step-by-step process can break it down to help you go after this right away.

At the end of this worksheet, you should understand the steps and factors for launching a gathering at your work and actually starting a meeting with people you have led to Christ, have discipled, and/or who are exploring faith in some way with you. This process has some similarities to launching a local marketplace multipliers chapter, so if you've already done that you've practiced some of the activities that will make this easier.

STEP 1—Get Advice from Others

Learn from others in your local chapter or connect with other marketplace multipliers in the ministry through MarketplaceMultipliers.com and the resources found there. There is no need for you to try to reinvent the wheel when it comes to doing this, and others who have been there before will be of great help.

STEP 2—Define the Purpose of Your Gathering

It is important from the start to clarify your purpose for gathering people at your work. Here are some of the many purposes such a gathering might have:

Outreach group—A safe group for those that are already Christians at your workplace to get together in a way that they can invite other coworkers to join them.

Bible study—A group that will go through a certain book of the Bible together like "Discovery Bible Study";* this group could include both Christians and non-Christians. It could also be centered on the same questions asked of a passage each week.

Book study—A group that focuses on studying a Christian leadership or apologetics-oriented book that is good for non-believers to read.

Microchurch—A group for Christians and non-Christians, intended to be a fresh expression of church in the workplace setting; it would include all core elements of church life.

Q&A group—An environment where non-Christians can pose any question they want to a few more seasoned Christians who either answer the questions or research them and come back with responses the following meeting.

Write here how you would describe the purpose of this new gathering in a text to someone you're inviting. You can also use this when you are sending invitations.

STEP 3—Make a List

Who would be the best people to invite into your gathering? Below is a space to write their names. To get you started, think of friends of yours:

Nones—Those who have no religious affiliation or say "none of the above" when asked.

Unchurched—Those who are unchurched but have some belief in Jesus Christ already.

Religious—Those who belong to a different religion, but would like to learn about Jesus.

Unsure—Those you have had some spiritual conversations with but who are unsure of where they stand.

Potential Disciples—Those you have led to Christ or who look to you for some spiritual wisdom from time-to-time that you can begin to disciple in this gathering.

360 Degrees—Those you work for (why not ask them to come, instead of just asking for permission to hold a meeting), those who work for you (clarify that you are not making them come), and your peers in the organization.

Leaders—Those who could help you lead.

Make a list of those people you might invite here:

STEP 4—Pray

The first thing to do with your list is to pray over your names. Pray that God would move in the hearts of those you are going to reach out to, and work "before you" in their lives to prepare the way.

Thank—Be grateful to God for each of the people on your list. Thank God for the opportunity to participate in the Great Commission in this way.

Ask—Make requests of God for the lives of those on your list. Ask God to give you wisdom as you start this marketplace gathering.

Praise—As opportunities arise to connect with those on your list, give God praise. Praise God for the love and truth he has shown you.

Write out a short two- to three-sentence prayer for wisdom in starting your marketplace gathering:

STEP 5—Partner

It may be helpful to find someone to partner with you in starting this marketplace gathering. By not "going it alone" and sharing the facilitation duties, it can lessen the weight on your shoulders. It can also help the group be consistent in meeting regularly even if you happen to be out of town at a scheduled meeting time. If you have a partner, they can lead without you there.

Write down names of people with whom you might meet with to discuss your dreams for this marketplace gathering and ask if they might partner with you in leading it:

STEP 6—Plan

Think through how your marketplace gathering will work. Where will you meet? How many people do you expect, minimum and maximum? Will you serve refreshments? Tea and coffee? Will you ask anyone to bring anything? How will you guide the discussion?

If you don't yet know what to do when you meet, here is a helpful starting plan that is revised from the "Discovery Bible

Study" disciple-making process.* These are questions you can ask at every meeting to keep it as simple as possible:

- What happened in the last week that you are thankful for?
- What struggles are happening in your life, family, or community?
- What struggles can we pray for?
- What did you learn last time we got together?
- How did it go in living out what you learned?

Read the Bible together or listen to the audio or video version of a Bible passage.

- Can you retell any parts of the passage in your own words?
- Are there any other details anyone found to be important?
- What do we learn about God and people in this passage of the Bible?
- How would your life change if you obeyed and lived out what you are learning here?
- Who would you like to tell this part of the Bible to and how are you connecting with them?
- How can we help meet needs in your life?

STEP 7—Schedule

Figure out what day or night of a typical week works best for you to schedule your meetings. What's the best time not just for you, but for the people you want to include in this? Once this is scheduled, clear that in your calendar for several months. It is also important to find a starting date to launch with your first meeting. Be sure to get your partner or others you are inviting that are closest to you to commit to this date first.

STEP 8—Contact

It's time to reach out to those on your list with the details. Send texts and emails, preferably one-on-one, not groups, and make the invite. Some you may want to meet with face-to-face to make the invite, and others you could call. The key is to make this a personal invitation, not a general "Y'all come" on social media. Give each person the specific start and end times, address, and a sense of what the gathering will feel like. Be low-key with this invitation. It is not a huge deal and high pressure; it's just an invitation to gather with you for the purpose you indicate.

Part of this contact should start with "where they are at." What is it that will draw them to your gathering? It could be many things:

Community—Some are just looking for friendships and connection with others. They may feel lonely and you would be providing a safe place for them.

Curiosity—Some would like to learn more about Jesus, the Bible, and Christianity.

Depth—Some might already be Christians, but they want to go deeper into their faith and not just listen to others talk about it.

Questions—Some might have specific questions that they are hoping to find answers for.

Problems—Some have problems unique to their lives and they are searching for solutions to those problems.

STEP 9—Start

Hold your first meeting and take note of what works well and what you can do better next time. The good thing is that this small meeting is not a big deal and not everything rides on it. If the starting gathering isn't all that great, it's not the end of the world . . . you've got the next meeting scheduled!

This is another reason not to delay starting too long. It's better to just start and get going rather than wait. There is not a lot of risk to this kind of launch, so better to just dive in and figure it out along the way.

STEP 10—Practice

Practice makes perfect. Well, you're not quite aiming for perfection in your workplace gatherings, but you do want it to get better from week to week. After each meeting, reflect on how your gathering went and what you might like to do differently the next meeting. Nothing teaches like experience. Your context is different than that of others. Make little adjustments to how things go in order to improve from week to week.

STEP 11—Be Faithful and Fruitful

Your biggest job as marketplace gathering leader is to be a faithful friend and to encourage those on your list, whether they come to the marketplace gatherings or not.

Keep growing your list of those you are having spiritual conversations with. If you are a good friend, over time some will respond to your invitation to join the gatherings.

It will be key to just meet consistently and be a transforming presence in your workplace. There is something noble and trustworthy about being consistent in the lives of those on your list.

The fruit you are seeking from the seeds you plant may not come right away. It may take some time, but when you are faithful, over time God will give you the fruit he intends for you to harvest. You might plant seeds, others might water them, and still others may harvest them—but know that God is the one who makes everything grow. Trust God for that fruit. Enjoy the faithful and fruitful journey in God!

*For more information on the "Discovery Bible Study" process, see *Contagious Disciple Making: Leading Others on a Journey of Discovery* by David Watson and Paul Watson (Thomas Nelson: 2014).

ABOUT THE AUTHORS

This book contains the stories of more than a dozen marketplace multipliers, as told by them in recorded interviews. They seek to convey what it means to be the kind of Christian who intentionally integrates their faith and work to the benefit of those around them, making disciples and multiplying the kingdom of God. The bio of each multiplier is found at the end of their chapter.

David Drury is a multivocational second-chair leader, org founder, church planter, and author of more than ten books, including work as collaborating writer and lead editor of *Marketplace Multipliers*, coauthor of *God Is for Real* and *SoulShift: The Measure of a Life Transformed,* and author of *Transforming Presence: How Being with Jesus Changes Everything,* and *Being Dad*. David has been Max Lucado's personal researcher since 2005, chief of staff for The Wesleyan Church headquarters since 2012, a writing collaborator since 1999, and husband to Kathy since 1996. His work can be found at DavidDrury.com.